CESTUS

Racing The Ice To Cape Horn -- By Frank Guernsey & Cy Zoerner

Racing The Ice To Cape Horn

Frank Guernsey
Cy Zoerner

Editor: Carol-Faye Ashcraft

Bristol Fashion Publications
Harrisburg, Pennsylvania

Racing The Ice To Cape Horn -- By Frank Guernsey & Cy Zoerner

Published by Bristol Fashion Publications

ISBN: 1-892216-20-5
LCCN: 99-073126

We Gratefully Acknowledge The Following Contributions

Cover Photo by: Mary Guernsey
Cover Design by: John P. Kaufman
Interior Graphics by: John P. Kaufman
Author Photo -- Frank Guernsey by: Garrison Frost, Jr.
Author Photo Cy Zoerner by: Frank Matranga
Author Photo, Inside Back Cover by: Garrison Frost, Jr.

Dedication

To my wife, Mary.
Frank

To my wife, Laura.
Cy

Racing The Ice To Cape Horn -- By Frank Guernsey & Cy Zoerner

Prologue

The question "Why do people do what they do?" is endlessly fascinating, perhaps because its answer might tell us why *we* do what we do. For centuries philosophers, theologians, poets, artists, humanists, and more recently behavioral scientists have pondered the question.

Why would an ordinary person, an insurance salesman from Redondo Beach, California, turn from everyone he loves and alone face the terrors of the Southern Ocean in a quest that was almost sure to destroy him?

Why?

This book chronicles Frank Guernsey's fantastic race with the icebergs to Cape Horn. Even more it offers insights from his life that suggest the origins of his thirst for outlandish sea adventure.

Oceans aren't crossed without help, and I wish to thank the many people who helped me in acquiring, reinforcing, refurbishing and provisioning *Cestus*.

Racing The Ice To Cape Horn -- By Frank Guernsey & Cy Zoerner

Contents

Prologue   Page 9

Chapter One   Page 17
  Facing Fear at the Bottom of the World

Chapter Two   Page 25
  Committing to Cape Horn

Chapter Three   Page 35
  Sailing into Infinity

Chapter Four   Page 45
  Sailing on the Edge

Chapter Five   Page 55
  Springing a Leak Before Crossing the Line

Chapter Six   Page 63
  Countering the Counter-currents

Chapter Seven   Page 77
    Grasping at the Wind

Chapter Eight   Page 89
    Ghosting Through the Mentor Current

Chapter Nine   Page 99
    Reaching the Roaring Forties

Chapter Ten   Page 111
    Surviving "The Worst Storm Possible"

Chapter Eleven   Page 125
    Screaming Into the Screaming Fifties

Chapter Twelve   Page 139
    Outliving the Ultimate Storm

Chapter Thirteen   Page 151
    Running the Iceberg Line

Chapter Fourteen   Page 165
    Winning the Race

Chapter Fifteen   Page 179
    Dodging the Deadly Overfalls

Chapter Sixteen   Page 191
    Struggling up the Atlantic

Chapter Seventeen   Page 201
    Falling on a Stanchion

Chapter Eighteen   Page 213
Missing a Safe Port

Chapter Nineteen   Page 225
Arriving in Uruguay

Chapter Twenty   Page 235
Re-Entering the Human Race

About the Authors   Page 244

Chapter One

Facing Fear
At The Bottom Of The World

"Humans!"

The handle of my precious watermaker stopped in my hands. My eyes strained at the black speck on the gray, watery horizon. The misery from the open saltwater sores I sat on winked out. As I switched on my video recorder, my only companion since I set sail, I repeated, "Humans? After all these months alone..."

I glanced at my watch. It was January 2. 10 a.m.

In my excitement, the watermaker clanked onto the fiberglass cockpit floor, just missing my foot. I reached inside the cabin for binoculars. The glasses revealed hardly more than a faint dot, but across the placid, long swells, the dot had the vague shape of a boat.

"Yes!" I shouted into the desolation.

It was easy to anticipate the life aboard the oncoming ship -- a capable captain, a jolly crew, with heated cabins and the smells of hot food wafting from the galley -- spotting my small boat, coming to investigate, to see if they could give me assistance. They'd have warm, dry bunks, hot food, dry clothes, so much fresh water they could drink all they wanted, and probably even shower in it.

Their boat would cut through the water, unlike my craft, thrashing in every wave, sapping my energy just keeping my balance. I couldn't wait to see their smiling faces and waving hands, hear their surprised voices shouting. Truly an unlikely sight in these waters.

Though I wouldn't board, I'd certainly have a drink with these fellow mariners. Camaraderie here in this most enormous wilderness on earth would be sweet, human contact and all that human contact means. How I would love to hear human laughter again.

"No!"

Not after being so close in this great ocean.

Was it my eyes? Was the speck turning away?

Frantically, I keyed my tiny VHF marine radio.

"This is the sailing vessel *Cestus* out of Redondo Beach, California, calling the motor ship. Can you hear me?"

Only white noise. I knew my radio was working. I had talked with a lone Chilean close ashore only two days prior.

I desperately needed this vessel, because my tiny radio transmitted only line-of-sight, relatively few miles across this wilderness. I was aching to let my wife, Mary, and my family know I was still alive. Any boat except mine this far off the traditional course would carry powerful single sideband transmitters that could relay my messages back to the world.

"It's turning back. I think, it's coming this way." I was laughing, almost giddy. "Maybe he's a fisherman or maybe a naval vessel." Chilean or Argentine, probably, but it could be almost anyone.

Sighting the boat had broken my reverie. Trying to dry out from the heavy weather, I had relaxed, composing myself after stressful months of violent seas. Accustomed as it was to everlasting gales, the skin of my face felt almost numb in the calm. The agony of eroding skin, many saltwater sores, cuts, bruises, and aches -- inflicted by some of the most berserk seas on earth -- eased a bit as I basked in the pale sunlight.

It was a time of relief and recovery. I gazed into the water, seeing a stranger. The reflection revealed a gaunt face and a white beard. No doubt I had lost many pounds after months of mariner's fare. Visions of oranges, apples, bananas, lettuce, grapes, and melons tantalized me.

We rode the peaceful swells, the scions of a distant and forgotten storm. *Cestus* gently rose to the vast mounds that passed under, like a slow ride up a mountain, and my mind was flowing with it. Compared with yesterday, *Cestus* was a floating featherbed instead of a grinding concrete mixer. This was good, and a good place to be, in the sunlight, at the center of a giant, blue-gray ball, in ethereal time.

Lazily, I was thinking of the return of a sailing wind and the currents that would confront me on my future course. Ahead lay the Burdwood Bank, the Mintay Reef, and the alien Atlantic Ocean, alien at least to me, for decades a Pacific Ocean sailor. But for the moment I was at peace, pumping the watermaker, counting -- often miscounting -- each stroke between 500 and 800.

As I babbled to myself, the speck in the binoculars slowly transformed into a gray vessel of about 70 feet. It looked as if it meant business, a patrol boat or gunboat. Why was it advancing so deliberately? Was this to be an official visit?

On the one hand, I hungered for camaraderie, and I prepared for some kind of exchange. But there is also a down side to humans, and I was at the mercy of strangers. They could be coming to kill me. No one would ever know what became of me. Or was this only the paranoia of enforced solitude? "I hope this guy's not a pirate," I said to my video recorder.

The closer the boat came, the more my mouth and throat grew dry and, ironically, the more alone I felt. The stranger was armor-plated, and behind the gun slits, who knew what kind of weaponry lurked? Probably, at the least, fifty-caliber machine guns.

He might now be in radio range. "This is *Cestus* calling. Can you hear me?"

Not a sign of life aboard.

Involuntarily, I went on the alert. He was less than a mile away. Why wouldn't he respond? I tried again, this time in my tortured Spanish.

No reply.

"When you're alone out here, you just don't want to be approached by who you don't know. At least I don't," I said aloud, hearing a growing panic.

He circled me silently, ever tightening his arc. Was he simply curious, or was he stalking me? Why was he checking me out so carefully? My hope of contacting Mary died.

"He's not acknowledging my calls, as I sit here wondering..."

My heart pumped with the ancient rhythm of danger. In some primitive way, my perception focused with perfect clarity. No longer did I need the binoculars.

What did I have that anyone would want? My boat was a 31-year-old fiberglass sloop with water leaking into the sloshing bilge. *Cestus* was only an old sailboat, engineless, and worked from a long voyage in seas it was never intended to navigate. Absurd to think a pirate might want it for profit. But what about my food?

"I'm down to 38 meals," I said to the video recorder.

I had little confidence that my food would last to my intended port, Mar del Plata, Argentina. My most valuable piece of equipment was probably the PUR watermaker, which rendered sea water drinkable, but it would be ridiculous for this marauder to kill me for it.

No wind in my beard, no ripples on the water. The benevolent seas mocked me.

Removing the video camera from its mount, I taped the slow-moving, malevolent boat. I zoomed in closer. There was a good chance nobody would ever see this tape of the circling patrol boat, gunboat, pirate -- whoever -- or maybe any of the other tapes from my voyage.

I felt utterly helpless. And now it was clear that this ugly steel hulk posed another of the many obstacles in my path to safety.

"It's an uncomfortable feeling, but you have to deal with it."

Had I come this far, trying to reach an impossible dream, for nothing? My bottom lip cracked as I grinned at the irony. My iceberg enemies had been forming for millennia, waiting to crush me. Now, if I fell prey to this gunboat, they would be cheated.

Few people around the bar at the yacht club had given me much chance of survival. One said, "Frank, if you fight icebergs, the icebergs always win." At the time I had the sinking feeling she was right, even though I didn't exactly intend to "fight" the bergs. Who would ever know how far I had sailed in my quest before the end? Or was that even important now?

Yards from my boat, a large albatross paddled in the long swells. Like the Ancient Mariner, would I finally wear it around my neck? Near him were a dozen little black birds I couldn't identify. In this relative warmth, perhaps the sea birds congregated to mate. Maybe life and death floating along together.

"This is the sailing vessel *Cestus* ..."

He remained mute. Like the *Mary Celeste*, the gunboat

19

seemed abandoned. No waving hands. No smiling faces. But there was some intelligence guiding that helm. Was it evil?

The gun slits looked like dark slashes, but I couldn't see the guns. It was still possible he was a government patrol boat, but which government? I could see no flags, nor any other identification. One thing was sure: This was no fishing or commercial boat.

I began to sweat, almost unthinkable at 56^0 south latitude. I smelled of wet wool. The skies were serenely clear and the temperature was about 70^0 Fahrenheit, a typical day in my California home, but extremely rare this close to the South Pole and the "red line" of icebergs. By nightfall, I knew, the cold would return to pierce me. With luck.

The peaceful water slapped my calmly rocking craft. As the intruder circled closer, I heard the faint drone of diesels.

"I don't want any trouble," I said aloud, my voice imploring.

The closer he approached, the more terrifying he appeared. Was it possible his dark hull, white superstructure, businesslike gun slits and bristling antennae array added up to my last voyage?

The acrid diesel smoke was like an assault across the water. A confrontation was inevitable. Now there seemed only one course of action.

By nature, I am gentle. The last thing on my mind was killing, even in self-defense, but I wasn't going down without a struggle. I had a 12-gauge shotgun aboard, and a friend had provided ammunition before I sailed from King Harbor.

Maybe an old Cold War strategy would work. I'd show the shotgun and hope it would give him proper notice, provide a deterrent. Of course, it might provoke an attack. It was something like a match between an air rifle and a cannon. In any case, having the gun handy would provide a comfort.

He could blow me out of the water at will, or run me down. Up close, I might blast his hull, but would my 2 3/4-inch slugs, selected by a Los Angeles County deputy sheriff, penetrate the steel below the waterline?

Almost two hours had passed since he started stalking me. It was time for action. I couldn't run because of the calm, and there was no place to hide in this rolling isolation. I must be ready. Ridiculously outgunned, I must face whatever was in store. I reached below. The weapon felt cold in my bruised hands.

Inhaling his diesel fumes, I could almost hear the hammering gunfire as it shattered the Antarctic silence. I could feel myself sinking beneath the paralyzing, cold water, caught in the same current as my enemy icebergs.

Clack-clack. I injected a slug into my shotgun.

Racing The Ice To Cape Horn -- By Frank Guernsey & Cy Zoerner

Chapter Two

Committing To Cape Horn

What was I doing here at the bottom of the world, menaced by a silent, steel stranger in a gently rolling sea? Why did I trade everything I love for solitary Antarctic days and nights in which my breath clouded in front of my face while the batteries froze in my hand-held satellite navigation system?

What strange forces dropped me aboard a leaking daysailer -- only a few feet longer than the old Lincoln Continental I drove -- and into the Pacific Ocean, a vast wilderness of ninety-three million square miles, twice the size of the Atlantic, bigger than all the continents combined?

The answer was simple. Tuesday, August 28, 1990, when I was forty-eight years old, I promised myself I would sail alone and nonstop from Redondo Beach, California, around Cape Horn. Mary and I were separated, and I was living in a place I called "the Dungeon."

I'd made a commitment to myself: I would make this journey. The strange compulsion that drove me to such drastic ambitions would echo through my mind for the entire voyage. Committing to extensive ocean voyages requires an enormous amount of planning, work, expense, and worry. It was like being on a train gaining speed: No slowing. No stopping. No reversing. No turning. The steel rails dictated the future. And the tremendous weight of my commitment drove me inexorably forward toward my struggle in the Southern Oceans.

"Guernsey," said my longtime nemesis, Bruce, a denizen of King Harbor, "you're a maniac. The only reason you're trying this stunt is to draw attention to yourself. Why don't you go over Niagara Falls in a barrel or walk a tightrope between the top of tall buildings like an ordinary lunatic? It'd probably be safer."

The tone of his voice revealed that he was encouraging me, as always.

"I'm not an ordinary lunatic," I protested.

With that, Bruce replied, "Well then, you're going to try to set a record so you get your name in the record books."

It was true that if I made it, mine would be the smallest boat to sail nonstop from North America, around Cape Horn, to Uruguay. But I would claim no record of any kind. It would simply befall me with the voyage.

On that windless day in August when I made the commitment, if someone had asked why, I would have responded that thirst for adventure and the experience drove me. And I would have meant it.

Cape Horn is the ultimate challenge for sea adventurers. It is the Everest of the oceans. If Everest is the top of the world, then Cape Horn at the far tip of South America is the bottom. Cape Horn was my personal Everest, and rounding it would be all the reward I would need.

I would have some idea of how my heroes, Nepalese Sherpa, Tensing Norkay and Sir Edmund Hillary, must have felt when they reached the 29,028-foot summit in 1953. If I could round Cape Horn, it would be like an ordinary guy climbing Everest without oxygen.

During the voyage, however, I'd discover this Mount Everest image was among the weakest spurs driving me.

But that August day, I was rich in experience, if poor in pocket. With two friends, I had sailed a 26-foot boat down the coast of Baja, California. More significantly, I had single-handed the same boat from my home port of Redondo Beach to Hawaii. Later, aboard a 24-foot wooden boat, I had made two single-handed voyages: first to Tahiti, and a few years later to Japan.

I knew the obstacles that awaited me on both land and sea, mile by sea mile. On land, I would be picking my way through a mine field on the way to the sea. The explosives were mostly financial and social.

All four voyages had prepared me for a try at Cape Stiff, as traditional sailors call it. Or so I thought.

I was to discover that no amount of experience can make a mariner a match for Cape Horn. Calms, violent storms, gales, giant, foaming, breaking seas, paralyzing cold, and lumbering icebergs lay in wait for me. But even before that, there were many hurtles ashore.

The most obvious was that I had no boat and little money to buy one. I had to find a potentially stout craft, buy it, rig it, and otherwise ready it for the supreme test.

I'd need a fortune to make it ready for what would prove to be a brutal voyage. I'd need people with the skills to reinforce it, probably rebuild it. How could I pay them? I had to launch the boat and rent a slip while I learned to sail it properly. In addition, I had to acquire some expensive equipment, even though I sail as simply as possible. I would need food and supplies to last for months, along with a self-steering vane and probably a new mast.

The cliché "a boat is a hole in the water into which you pour money" held true as I prepared. To make matters worse, I did not seek commercial sponsorship, for reasons I revealed to no one at the time, adding to my reputation for eccentricity.

Money, of course, wasn't the only mine in my road. Webs of restraints, spun from responsibilities, allegiances, and obligations, nail even loners like me to the shore. Freeing myself from the entanglements of humans had become no easier, even after several major voyages. Family and professional ties are the strongest. Because I'm an independent insurance salesman, I would have to retain my clients, even though many thought me involved in a hare-brained scheme. And someone would have to take care of business while I ventured at sea.

Even after all is in place, the single-hander simply trades land mines for sea mines. In my mind's eye, they are the devastating, dark mines, bristling with deadly nubs, launched by the Germans in World War I. No amount of money will stop the single-hander from colliding with these obstacles -- physical and mental.

At sea, the anxiety of running out of drinking water is as powerful as the fear of drowning. Humans can survive ten times longer without food than without water. If my freshwater maker malfunctioned, I would face a few more tortured and delirious days of life before succumbing to death from dehydration.

My spirit doesn't run out during a voyage, but my spirits do, inflicting additional hardship. Running out of brandy devastates my daily routine. My favorite ritual at sea is cocktail hour and I look forward to it all day.

Second only to water, food is a special concern. Whereas a modern watermaker doesn't take up much space aboard a small boat, food does. At first, it appears there is too much stuffed into all the nooks and crannies below, but as each day goes by, the food supply dwindles. It seems to disappear even faster when the solo sailor is becalmed and behind schedule. As the food supply plummets, anxiety soars.

Health complications pose another threat. I carry my basic first-aid kit and try not to think about breaking down physically or sustaining an injury I can't doctor myself.

Then there is time. Exacting time. I calculated that once a year -- and then for only one ten-day period -- the way around Cape Horn would be clear of icebergs at a time the weather and sea would permit the passage of my tiny craft. This would be in the Antarctic summer, at the time of our winter in California. Every mile of the way, I'd be in a deadly race with the icebergs.

Further calculation showed -- give or take a few days -- I would need 100 days of good sailing to reach the Cape. The key to survival, like the key to many things in this life, was to be at the right place at the right time. Every day would have to consume a specified distance. Getting there from California would probably be more hazardous than rounding Cape Stiff itself. Every day would be a mortal struggle with time.

Intensifying the struggle would be weather and sea conditions. There were confusing equatorial currents and counter-currents to navigate, dead spots in the sea devoid of wind, challenging because the boat was motorless, winds piping to sixty knots, seas that were tumbling mountains, overfalls, and contrary winds.

Cape Horn is notorious for the worst storms in the world. Later when I read Sebastian Junger's "The Perfect Storm," I realized that many of the seas he so aptly described would be at home off the primordial Cape. Murderous storms have destroyed sailing ships since the time of Magellan. Though modern ships fare better, the danger of the seas off the Cape were among the reasons the United States built the Panama Canal.

Pilot charts indicate that during December, Force 8 winds -- 37 to 44 knots -- are blowing an average of one day in every four. When the gales blow across the relatively shallow water, the waves increase to fifty feet. Most manufacturers design boats the size I planned to use for 15 knots of wind but no small boat is designed to withstand this beating from wind and wave.

I knew I would face mental as well as physical challenges. Prolonged terror drains me in spirit as well as body. My greatest dread at sea is being run down by freighters or other ships, or striking something like a sleeping whale or an awash cargo container, strayed from the deck of a dry bulk carrier. I fear being awakened by pounding engines just outside the fiberglass skin of my vessel. A ship running me down would be like a locomotive running over a penny. No one aboard the ship would notice. I would be only one of about sixty-five vessels a year -- lost without a trace.

Less dangerous but equally as vexing is confinement, being prisoner in a fiberglass cell. I thrive on physical exercise and rely on a daily run down the beach to keep me fit. The cockpit of my small sailboat will measure about nine feet long by six feet at the widest point, not exactly a gymnasium, and the cabin will barely provide space for sitting upright. Amazingly, adjusting to the eternal movement of the boat, the constant changing of sails, and pumping a watermaker by hand all afford good physical exercise.

Reading helps me keep my mind off the confinement and provides mental exercise. Although physically confined aboard my small boat, my mind can travel to the far reaches portrayed within the pages.

From experience, I knew two kinds of madness stalk the single-hander. First is suspected madness before and after the voyage. The second is the real thing, bobbing through the water.

Suspected madness is a deterrent to voyaging alone because large numbers of people ashore will conclude the solitary sailor must be insane to make hazardous ocean passages in a small boat. Upon hearing of my voyages, the first reaction of most people is, "He must be crazy." But planning and executing a successful single-handed voyage provides an exercise in rationality and logic well beyond the ability of the everyday madman. Or so I tell myself.

Solitude -- being alone for months and exposed to overwhelming natural forces -- is a freeway to madness. A recurring question put to the single-hander is, "How can you bear the loneliness?"

The real madness to fear is snapping during a voyage and wandering over the sea until dying of thirst, starvation, shipwreck, sinking, or collision.

Storms sometimes continue in time and intensity beyond my endurance. They shake the foundations of my sanity, and I must admit that a number of times at sea, I've looked over the brink of lunacy. As I later watch videos of my extended voyages, I can see a madman slowly emerging, though it may only be my lengthening beard, my haggard face, and my strained, hollow eyes.

All these mines lurked between me and my goal. Striking any one of them could destroy my dream. Striking one at sea could destroy me. But anticipating these obstacles lifted me from the quagmire of the mundane insurance business, the stinging, smog-filled eyes, the 24-hour auto alarms, and day-to-day drudgery of life ashore.

The price of freedom is to push on and avoid the explosives in your path. With true excitement, I began the search for my boat.

* * * * * * * * *

After finding *Cestus*, I had borrowed on my life insurance to push on. Over the next 42 months, I sank every penny into the resurrection of my little sailboat. To make it competitive in racing icebergs, the boat had to be re-engineered. Almost everything had to be replaced to give me a chance in tremendous, breaking seas.

Without the help of Bob Cringan, Ron Watt, and Kevin Ryan, I'd still be slaving away in the Ace Storage yard. I hired Cringan and Watt because they are friends and because they are good shipwrights. Graciously, without charge, they contributed many extra hours and ideas.

Kevin Ryan is a first-class rigger, an expert in the selection, installation, and adjustment of all the wire cables aboard. Years younger than I, he was a formidable sailor who raced successfully at the King Harbor Yacht Club.

Doggedly, we worked through the tasks. We designed and fabricated a new steel rudder, cut out holes to lighten it, and fiberglassed the whole assembly. A sound rudder is the most essential part of the steering system.

For maximum strength, we replaced the chainplates and bolted them through the hull. The chainplates are the attachment points for the portion of the wire rigging called shrouds. The shrouds keep the mast upright from side to side and the chainplates hold the shrouds in place.

We did much of the work from scratch because many original parts were missing and we had no patterns. We installed a compression post, a vertical post inside the cabin, to reinforce the foredeck, which would be plunging through cold, sledgehammering seas. We replaced both hatches, the doors into the cabin, to increase strength and to keep out as much water as possible.

To create a storage compartment, we fiberglassed the bottom of the outboard motor well. We wouldn't need the well because *Cestus* would carry no engine. We built a locker in the cockpit to hold the propane for my stove. We decided the bulkhead, a wall perpendicular to the hull running across the hull, needed no reinforcement.

We installed a new, sturdy (and expensive) mast and the device that attached its base to the deck. Ed Taylor, now retired, at T&A Sails in Wilmington, California, cut crisp, new sails and repaired the old genoa jib, the largest of the forward sails but used only once during the voyage. *Cestus* sported a new mainsail with triple reefing points, a new reefing working jib, a new small storm jib. The original main and jib served as backups. The addition of reefing points allow the sails to be lowered and secured to reduce sail area. In essence, this made one sail into four different-size sails.

Carefully, we replaced all the hardware that helps with raising and lowering the sails and adjusting their shape to match varying winds.

We changed all the electrical wiring so I could display running lights, even though they would be useless most of the time. We anticipated a swamped cockpit and upgraded the drains to clear it.

Ron Watt came up with a sound idea. "That cabin is going to be cramped." He continued. "You'll be blind down there and won't be able to see what's happening on deck. In a blow, that'd really be dangerous. Why don't I make a little doghouse so you can see better?"

It was true that the flush-decked *Cestus* left scant room for my nearly six feet of height. Ron fabricated a permanent doghouse on top of the hatch. The doghouse was simple, a small box with windows that would permit me to stick my head up to watch the sails, weather, and sea conditions from the relative security and warmth of the cabin.

It wasn't artistic, and its flat sides probably offered more wind resistance than a dome would have, but it turned out to be one of the most useful modifications we made. Not only did the doghouse relieve confinement, but it also kept me out of the weather. Wind and sea spray create fatigue, a sailor's mortal enemy, and the doghouse protected me from both.

For the same reason, self-steering was more important this time than on previous voyages. I simply couldn't remain in the cockpit and at the helm for more than four months.

The self-steering vane consisted of a paddle that caught the wind and a mechanism that transferred information from the paddle to the rudder. When attached to the stern of a boat, it would use the prevailing wind to steady the boat on its course, determined by setting the mechanism. The price of the vane was exactly $1,000 more than the price of the boat, but it was a crucial piece of equipment on a long passage. Bob Cringan helped mount it.

Thousands of tasks accumulated on my ubiquitous lists, and for the next three and a half years, I spent all my spare time ticking them off. My confidence in *Cestus* grew as we finished each task. Then, on September 4, 1992, in King Harbor, we were ready to launch.

Shortly afterward, I scheduled our maiden voyage, navigating from my slip to the King Harbor Yacht Club. I had purchased a 5 horsepower Nissan outboard motor for the occasion.   I admit to being more sailor than engineer, and somehow the outboard got cocked the wrong way, overpowered the steering, and before I knew what was happening, it drove me into three boats parked in their slips. No damage, but I left notes anyway.

My second time out of the slip was even more embarrassing. Mary and my cousin Di shared the cockpit with me. Mary and I had reconciled and she really belonged aboard because she was the catalyst for my voyaging. Pouring drinks to mark the occasion, we began motoring out of the harbor. Then, under the watchful eyes of many spectators from the King Harbor Yacht Club, I rammed a steel bait barge, sending Mary flying over the doghouse.

Fortunately, neither Mary nor my cousin was hurt. Although the doghouse wasn't damaged, poor *Cestus* suffered a watermelon-sized hole in the bow. This added little to my credibility as a sailor. An old fisherman on the nearby breakwater raised his wine glass to salute my buffoonery. The gestures from the yacht club members weren't so cordial. Thankfully, the puncture was above the waterline and spared us a sinking.

By the time Ron Watt repaired and reinforced the bow by fiberglassing a massive piece of wood in place, *Cestus* was a far more rugged boat.

At long last, Kevin Ryan and I took *Cestus* out for sea trials, and it sailed like a dream. Unfortunately, nobody was watching.

Cestus now breathed with the robust life of a sturdy,

oceangoing vessel, or so I believed. Kevin's fine-tuning had made the little sloop as ready for the Southern Oceans as it would ever be.

Racing The Ice To Cape Horn -- By Frank Guernsey & Cy Zoerner

Chapter Three

Sailing Into Infinity

The band kicked into a raucous version of "Born to be Wild," and the voices escalated to a happy shout. Still, the band, the shouting, the laughter, the free-flowing booze and the camaraderie failed to lift my spirits during my going-away party.

One of the live-aboards from the harbor patted my shoulder. "Well, now that you've had this party, you'll have to go," he said with a grin. I knew he was right. I had been living in a kind of foggy no-man's-land for days.

I took a deep draught of beer. My friends seemed more

worried about Cape Horn than they had about my earlier crossing to Japan. I felt as if I were in a coffin, watching mourners at an Irish wake.

True, my will was made out and my life insurance was in order. Doubtless, a number of guests believed they'd never see me again, that this time Frank Guernsey had gone too far, taken on more than he could handle.

Even so, how could I not bask in the good will? I felt like a grouch for not wanting this party. Mary, a fantastic party giver, did want this party, and it was one of her best. She did much of the cooking, and the rest was potluck, a tradition at the Redondo Beach Yacht Club.

Across the room, my son, Frank, now in his early twenties, blended easily into the scene. He had readily agreed to help run my business during my absence and had quickly grasped the fundamentals.

The clubhouse was packed to the gunwales. Colorful flags from dozens of other boating clubs decorated our ceiling.

This was a modest club as yacht clubs go, and usually I could relax and be comfortable here in its informality. But not tonight. Somebody put another beer in front of me, and I drained it.

People pushed forward, shook my hand, and shouted things I couldn't hear, but I knew their good wishes went with me. Snippets of conversation floated my way. "OJ will never be brought to trial, not the Juice. He's too popular." There were moans all around.

My father tried to help. "Be a lionhearted bastard, Frank," he advised from his seat beside me. "Don't forget you have some brave ancestors with seafaring blood."

Are single-handers born, not made, I wondered?

I think not.

In the crowd, I saw doubters and defenders. The doubters believed I'd never round Cape Horn, never get near it in my small craft. Others probably believed I'd sail down the Baja somewhere, wait for a few months, sell the boat, and return to Redondo Beach, a fake hero.

Tony Williams, an older man with sea-blue eyes and an English accent, shook my hand and said, "As long as Frank Guernsey is alive, I'll know the human spirit prevails." Later, I learned he had been in the British navy for nine years during and after World War II.

Clustered in a corner were nearly a dozen defenders, my fellow members from the Adventurers' Club of Los Angeles, a fraternity of the daring. Each was recognized for exploits that would match any of mine.

I was about to join them when a smiling woman put a big rum and Coke in front of me, and I settled back to sample it and watch the crowd. Mary was having a good time with her friends and wasn't noticing me.

Only about half the partiers were sailors. There were also my associates from the insurance business and even some of my clients, who had helped prepare the boat.

Someone I didn't know lurched up with a tall glass of vodka on the rocks, and I accepted it gratefully.

Thankfully, the band took a break and conversation was possible again.

"How you doing, Frank?" my dad asked. He probably suspected I was drinking too much.

"Mom's not here," I observed.

There was no response.

A group of friends from high school days seemed to be having a happy reunion. I wanted to join them, but I was having a hard time getting up.

I watched them from my chair, especially my friend Carl Bono. After several strokes in his 40s, Carl looked vacant and destroyed, even though he still reminded me of the stocky Rocky Marciano type he once had been.

Our friendship reached back to Van Nuys High School, when we were about 16. Carl was one of the bravest men I had ever known though he never flaunted it. Carl, who would always stand up for a friend, was incapable of walking away from a confrontation.

All these years of friendship had brought Carl to my going-away celebration, knowing it would be his last party. My thoughts drifted back to those younger days.

One day we were cruising around in my blue 1951 Olds 98. It was a "cool" car, a teenager's delight with a V-8 the size of a Cadillac's, double exhaust pipes peeping out ahead of the rear tires, the front end dumped to give it a raked look. We decided to stop and pick up our buddy, Eddie Mathews. Next door to Eddie lived "Horrible Hank," a run-of-the-mill bully, but older than we were, in his early 20s. Beefy and powerful, Hank sat around on his mother's porch all day drinking beer with other drop-outs.

Carl, an amiable guy, called, "Hey, Daddy, have a beer!" Hank squeezed his Budweiser can and squirted a geyser into the air. Standing and flinging the can aside, Hank had all the excuse for a fight that any bully needs. He charged off the porch, happy that Carl was standing his ground on Eddie's lawn. Hank threw a roundhouse right, and ducking under it, Carl pitched his own right to the belly.

Much to Horrible Hank's embarrassment, Carl, though beaten and bloody, was still standing after 20 minutes.

Though Hank had the size and strength, Carl had the heart. And the bully was looking for a way out.

My father brought me back. "Why don't you circulate among your friends, Frank? I'm all right here."

"Do you know why Mom didn't come?" I asked.

He shook his head. "Too busy, I guess." My father studied the back of his frail hands.

My earliest memory flooded into my head. I was escaping from this man's house, standing on the sidewalk and longing to cross Harvard Street. It was midmorning and already the smog billowed among the trees with the kind of back-lighted mist that decorated Hollywood movies in those days. The sound of tires on the hot pavement beckoned. Standing on that hard sidewalk -- on my own -- was exciting.

Scarcely taller than the tires of the cars whizzing by, I felt the beginning of the world was just across the street, the world of excitement, the world of freedom to go and do as I pleased.

The cars flowed in a dangerous stream, but if I could run fast enough, I could make it through the occasional breaks in traffic and escape into the world, away from the unsettled household of parents and the confines of walls. I was curious, wondering what the people did and why.

Looking one way and then the other, I saw a break in the traffic. My little body tensed, ready to dash for independence.

"Frank!"

Suddenly, a giant lifted me from behind and carried me unceremoniously out of the sunshine and back into the stifling household prison.

At 80, my father was no longer a giant. He had been a salesman like me, though I would never reach the levels of sales he had. It would be more accurate to say I was a salesman like him.

People shook my hand and smiled and wished me luck. "You'll need it, buddy. Hang in there."

I stood with my back to the lighted trophy case and envisioned towering seas. Instead of wind whining in the shrouds, I could hear some of the yacht-club psychologists arguing about my reasons for sailing.

"He's using a boat rather than a gun," one argued primly.

"No way," countered another. "It's hormonal imbalance. His mid-life crisis is taking a weird direction, that's all."

Time slipped. I was withdrawing.

"The party's over, Frank." I looked into Mary's beautiful face. She put her arm around me and laid her head on my chest. A few people were hanging on to the bar, but the clubhouse, now with a sad, partied-out look, was almost empty.

* * * * * * * * * *

I shoved *Cestus* out of the slip and stepped aboard. Sweat ran down my temples. Despite this hot, humid, late-September day, I knew winter would soon chill this hemisphere, and summer would arrive at Cape Horn.

Under a bright and cheerful sky, my guts wrenched as I took the tiller. There was no evidence of wind. The steam over the power plant across from the harbor rose straight up, not a cat's paw ripple on the water, not a ruffling flag. Ghosting down King Harbor, I took in every detail of the rusty bait barge, the harbormaster's wooden office, the huge mural of California gray whales on the walls of the Edison plant, the Portofino Inn with late tourists preening on their balconies, the eternal brown pelicans on the breakwall, the playful sea lions stealing the catch of the local fishermen, and the large Redondo Beach tourist pier. Finally, *Cestus* caught the faint animation of Santa Monica Bay.

This was my first experience sailing alone aboard my Gladiator. I knew in the calm I would need my biggest foresail, the genoa. In the 12,000 miles that lay ahead, never again would the lack of wind dictate so large a sail.

Early that morning, I had decided, there was no point waiting. Emotionally, I was run down from the final preparations and farewells. Leaving now would put me within my ten-day time frame at the bottom of the world. And it was simply time to go.

The month since the party had been a neurotic, obsessive time. My eyes would fly open at 4 a.m. I would dress, steal out of the house into the darkness, and go to the boat. There were hundreds of last-minute tasks. I pored over my to-do lists feverishly, as condensation formed on the fiberglass.

Later in the day, I would struggle with setting up my business to run smoothly in my absence.

Earlier, on September 1, a local newspaper had published an article entitled "Going it alone: R. B. sailor plans trip of a lifetime." This was the only media notice of my departure. The article noted, "Guernsey was hesitant to tell his story. He didn't want to be pictured as some sort of swashbuckling hero, braving the high seas in search of glory."

Of *Cestus* the article noted, "The boat he will sail is not the first boat in King Harbor that anyone would pick for such a trip. It is an old Gladiator hull that he salvaged and strengthened for long-range sailing. It doesn't look like much from the outside but below deck it reveals itself to be a battleship in sloop's clothing."

On the morning of my departure, Mary and I ate breakfast at one of our favorite beach cafes, but I could only push my eggs around the plate. Even though we were back together, our last days hadn't been cheerful. Mary knew my time had arrived, and when I asked her to drive me to the boat, she wasn't surprised.

As we clung to each other at the dock, I knew she was thinking of one of her favorite, beautiful sayings, "I will see you again when we are golden clouds on the wind."

One of the few precious people in my life walked away. Despite my confidence, I knew this might be my last touch and smell and sight of her. The last time I'd hear her sweet voice.

I busied myself getting on with it. At the marina office, I shook hands with Kevin, whose look said it all. He didn't expect to see me again. I blinked back tears. Returning to *Cestus* was something like a walk to the gas chamber.

After all the hassle of preparation, I planned to stop at Avalon on Catalina Island for a day of rest before embarking for Cape Horn. Though the San Pedro Channel can funnel gales, it offered only light airs and long, slow-moving swells from the southwest as I sailed for Avalon. At times the wind stilled, and it was hard to see how *Cestus* could inch forward.

Pop-pop, pop-pop. The sails slatted from side to side as we rocked in the calm water.

By sunset, stalled two miles out of Avalon Harbor, I resorted to rowing, without success. I was exhausted. If my rowing system represented the rest of my preparation, we'd never reach Mexico, much less Argentina.

At last, a large sailboat motored up behind me. The skipper, the brother of a yacht club member, cheerfully threw me a line and yelled, "Hey, Frank, you'll be out here all night. Grab a tow."

Aboard were his wife and another couple.

Thirty minutes later, the harbormaster's employee took over in the dark to tow *Cestus* to a can buoy. As I tied on, the lights of Avalon reflected in the still water. This late in the season, there were few tourist boats in the fairy-tale harbor.

My benefactor yelled, "You owe me a bottle of scotch!" It's rude to offer help and then wisecrack about repaying the favor. It's simply not done at sea, and I foolishly obsessed about that breach of sea etiquette for weeks into my voyage. Obviously, a measure of my emotional state.

I did last-minute shopping ashore the next day. Running my fingers over rows of Campbell's soup was my last feeling of abundance. For months, my life would be based on scarcity.

That afternoon, I drank beer alone in a bar until I cried out of sheer emotion and relief. Luckily, the town was almost deserted and a seasoned bartender served me. At dinner, the only other customers were a friendly couple, and I shared my tale of humiliation over the demand for a bottle of scotch, then escaped to *Cestus* without making a complete fool of myself.

Early the next morning, I repacked my food, disarrayed even by the light-air crossing. I went ashore for breakfast, painfully aware that this might mark the last time my feet would ever touch land. It was Friday, September 23.

Sailing in or out of Avalon Harbor was forbidden because of the potential for collision with moored boats, so I had arranged for a tow out of the harbor. The harbormaster employs skilled boatmen, but the exit was not without mishap. As the towboat moved slowly forward, I tangled the mooring line around my $3,000 steering vane and tweaked it.

The towboat set me free in an accommodating wind, and a great sense of relief settled aboard *Cestus*.

One mile out and over 8,000 from Cape Stiff, the 100-

day countdown clock started ticking. This was the culmination of several years of work and anxiety. Without regret, we were offshore at last, steering to windward of San Clemente Island, a few miles to the south.

A Navy reserve, San Clemente Island is off-limits to yachtsmen without permission. Inadvertently, we sailed through some kind of ominous naval exercise, complete with dark-gray helicopter carriers, their offspring scurrying overhead, and missile frigates. The Navy probably wasn't pleased, but there was nothing we could do except sail on.

Slowly, San Clemente Island dropped behind us, our last sight of land for 100 days ... if all went well.

My thoughts drifted to Carl Bono. A day after the party he had yet another stroke, more severe than those before, and about a week after that I visited him. Still reminding me of Rocky Marciano, he was blind and semicomatose. Holding his hand, I felt he knew me. Hard to believe brave and jovial Carl had come to this.

Life is uncertain. As *Cestus* heeled to the west wind, I wondered which one of us would go first, Carl or me?

Racing The Ice To Cape Horn -- By Frank Guernsey & Cy Zoerner

Chapter Four

Sailing On The Edge

The thirteenth day out was as mild as the day Ahab struck his first whale. *Cestus* romped along with a pod of dolphins, silver torpedoes crisscrossing before our bow.

The dark clouds on the horizon unsettled me because I didn't want a repeat of yesterday's terror.

The sea had tested us for the first time with a real gale, brutal winds 34 to 40 knots and waves towering 18 feet. Technically, it would be a force 8 on the Beaufort Scale. The roaring wind and sea had repeatedly fetched me from the relative security of the cabin onto the bucking deck. I had no choice. I had to reef the main sail time and time again, lowering it, reducing the sail area.

The gale had made me wonder how long the boat could stand up to it. Or how long I could take it. At times, we were broadside to the seas, feeling helpless and thinking of what the next four months promised.

The gale made me forget, at least temporarily, the rash that had developed on my backside. What caused the pain? Saltwater? Sitting on fiberglass? Change of diet?

Cortisone ointment hadn't fazed it.

But the gale was over, and I shook out a reef by raising the sail to its full height. Graceful as gull wings, the white sails took a perfect curve against the blue sky. The gentle wind through my emerging beard reminded me that *Cestus* and I had survived. My wife and my son would like to know that. Sometimes I felt guilty for putting other people through the anxiety of my ocean passages. But my family understood my commitments. It made life as a single-handed sailor much easier.

I made a thorough check. So far, so good. Even though the damaged self steering vane had disengaged nine times the first day I repaired it with a bungee and it had been working well for almost two weeks. I christened it "Leo."

A few days ago, I had noticed sea water was seeping in, leaving the hull a little damp.

Already out of cranberry juice, I was shocked at how quickly my food supply was disappearing.

I wondered if the Filipino skipper of the freighter I had contacted by VHF two days before had relayed my message to my family. He had sounded friendly enough.

That freighter was more amiable than the ship that chased me on the third night out of Catalina. We'd tack one way, and the ship would steer after us; then we'd tack the other way and again it would follow as though he was trying to run me down. This scary game lasted long enough almost to unhinge me. The rest of the night I was awake every hour, peering into the darkness.

On the horizon, more dark clouds gathered. But I was sailing serenely with the main at the first reef and the jib reefed. This was a good combination and *Cestus* was balanced and comfortable. Any weather at all and we'd have to reef the sail down again. I listened to the hull and the water trading secrets. The sun gladdened my skin as I relished the excitement and purity of having survived at sea once again.

As I did each morning, I read passages from the Old Testament, loving the poetry and the spirituality.

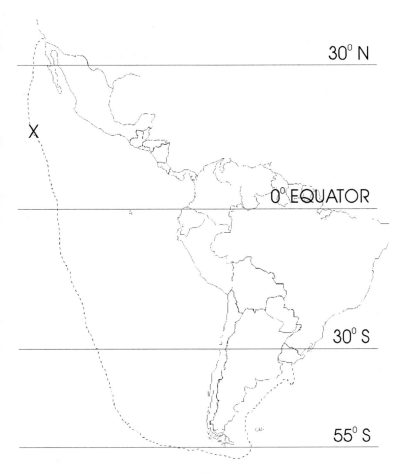

30° N

X

0° EQUATOR

30° S

55° S

Approaching the equatorial changes, we were at about 16^0 North latitude and 122^0 West longitude. Good progress, almost 100 nautical miles per day, on this our thirteenth day. The countdown of days remaining: 87. We were being pushed west a little, but I was willing to sacrifice direction now for comfort, such as it was. Pitcairn Island, home of the Bounty mutineers, lay to the southwest at 24^0 South and 130^0 West. Somewhere east and south of there, I wanted to turn toward Chile. In that area, the current begins to bend south and I could begin my run for Cape Horn. Today confirmed my belief that after every storm a good day will come. *Cestus* went about its business and the self-steering suggested a ghostly pilot aboard. I thought of Joshua Slocum, the first man to sail around the world alone. When he was feverish, he believed that the ghost of Columbus' pilot steered the *Spray*.

A dolphin leaped and for a magic second was suspended in the sunlight. Though I'm not superstitious, I do take dolphins as a good omen. I can't remember ever seeing them in heavy weather.

As the skies turned darker, *Cestus* continued to frisk along with the dolphins. As usual, their playfulness and intelligence buoyed my spirits.

But I was beginning to feel the effects of the voyage already. With the heat, I felt as if I were sailing in a cauldron. My forehead was sunburned but, worse, the top of my head was cut and raw. The gale had tossed me around like a rag doll inside *Cestus*. Bolts we had failed to trim off protruded from the deck into the cabin, slashing my skin as I bounced about.

Determined to stay healthy, I took my first complete shower. The tepid, fresh water whisked the stickiness from my skin, cleansing the saltwater deposits. No matter how delicious a shower can be ashore, there's nothing to match the pleasure of a freshwater shower after thirteen days at sea.

But I watched with anxiety as the water in my plastic bottles diminished, because I didn't understand how the watermaker worked. A 24-foot boat can't carry enough water for a five-month voyage, so I'd be forced to start using my desalinator when my water dwindled to two gallons.

If that didn't work, I might be able to reach some port. Once I started to use it, I had to continue or the filters would have to be changed. The manual made changing filters look like a mystical process far beyond my limited mechanical ability. I resolved to try the desalinator soon.

I considered the sea and sky. If I had a barometer aboard, it probably would be falling rapidly, but a barometer was a victim of priorities. By the time I paid for everything else, I had no money left for one. For the same reason, I carried a 20-year-old, single-chamber life raft. The money for a proper raft paid my federal and state taxes instead.

I prayed for no further gales. My wake trailed out like a temporary slash in the sea as *Cestus* held on course. Today, my life was what landsmen dream sea life to be. Effortless sailing, escorted by dolphins through a magical sea. For excitement, a threat of weather. Far offshore, away from human vexations. Clean and well fed.

To complete the picture, I fetched my flute from below. Playing it has been my custom since voyaging to Japan six years before. The flute passes the time and soothes me until I'm lost in the rhythm of the great ocean.

As I played "Yesterday" by the Beatles, I watched a dark cloud tower into the tropical sky and form an anvil at its peak. *Cestus* rocked along peacefully.

I was more fatigued than usual from thirteen days of sailing. Perhaps my 52 years were showing. Perhaps the four years since I made this commitment had not been as kind to me as I had thought. Before, when I had sailed, I had felt exuberance for several days, followed by a weariness from getting used to the marine environment, the exhausting wind and constant motion. The flute strayed from my lips as I nodded.

Rousing from my reverie, I searched the horizons. The darkening skies upset me, and the seas roiled with more energy.

Maybe foul weather was on its way again. I'd have time for some rest, but with one eye open. I went below to lie down. *Cestus* sang through the ocean.

I thought of my family, then reached for a book. It was my saltwater-soaked and ragged copy of Dumas, who wrote *Alone through the Roaring Forties.* Dumas enjoyed being away from crowded, smoggy cities like Los Angeles. Yes, it was good to be free -- away from society's requirements and restrictions and rules. It was good to leave the conventions of society and dare to make the ultimate run to Cape Horn.

I felt infinitely happy just living for the day, having the adventure, fulfilling the commitment. For companions I had dolphins, birds, music, reading, and cocktail hour. No smog here. The air smelled as if it had blown all the way from Hawaii.

Soon, it was time for cocktail hour in the cockpit while waiting for sunset. Aboard, sunset was almost a sacrament. It was the time of day for beauty, for feeling part of something eternally bigger than myself.

The western sky held myriad reds and golds. Daytime had turned beautiful. Even though the sea was coming up, we continued making progress. While I prepared dinner on my propane cooker inside the cabin, I succumbed to the sunset.

I switched on the tape player and "Diamonds and Rust" by Joan Baez wafted across the water. I enjoyed my dinner of cabbage and dressing, knowing it wouldn't last much longer.

Later, I lay down to read. The pain from my rash subsided, the print on the page swam, and my eyes closed.

Somewhere under the cockpit, I heard a chattering and wondered if we had rats aboard. I smiled in the dark at that impossibility. Even if there were rats, they certainly would have deserted the ship last night. The building seas needed minding, but my body relaxed after a fine day. Thinking of Mary, I fell asleep to dream.

I saw a frightened little boy in short pants, holding his father's hand and climbing the steps of a large, white frame house. He was only five years old. "You're going to like it here,

Frank," my father said.

A large woman with gray hair answered the door. "I'm Mrs. Sullivan," she said, "and you must be little Frank. We're going to play lots of games and learn lots of things here at my school. Won't that be fun?"

Was he going to leave me here?

What had I done so wrong that my mother and father wanted to leave me here with this stranger? What could it be? Did I make too much noise? Did I get too dirty? Did I refuse to eat everything they wanted me to? A burning feeling made me think I'd wet my pants. Then he really would leave me.

Before I could promise not to do any of those bad things again, we entered a large parlor.

"You'll like the other children. You'll make lots of friends, and you'll have a bed and locker all of your own. Won't that be nice?" my father asked.

He put the cardboard box with my things down on an old-fashioned couch. I could feel his grip on my hand weakening.

Despite the warm Santa Ana wind outside, the house felt chilled and I shivered.

* * * * * * * * * *

I came fully awake when a giant wave swatted *Cestus* onto its beam, dumping me onto the floor.

In the dark I felt the force of 2,050 pounds of lead ballast trying to right *Cestus*. We were lying flat, and the boat seemed slow in righting itself. A wave struck with the sound and force of a hundred sledgehammers, but with water sousing the hold, we struggled upright.

To control the situation, I had to reduce the sail immediately before the boat capsized or submerged. I found my safety harness and snapped it on, then struggled out into the cockpit. The world was pitch-black; the wind was shrieking around me.

The valleys between the rising seas provided tiny respites, but as the waves rolled under and we crested the peaks, the gale slammed us and we came close to swamping.

In the dark I found and loosened the main sheet, the line holding the main sail's boom, and *Cestus* eased. Alarmingly, the tether to my harness tangled in the lines and cables, intensifying an already dangerous situation by slowing my movements. I vowed never to wear it again.

Should I let *Cestus* run under bare poles or try to maintain control and use the sail? I tied in a double reef.

As best I could judge from the pitching deck, the seas were fifteen to twenty feet, and winds were 40 knots or more.

"Be a lionhearted bastard, Frank," I shouted to the unseen clouds cooking overhead.

Desperately, I lowered the jib, tied in a reef, and hoisted the jib sail again. The gale drove *Cestus* like a bullet before it.

I heard what sounded like an approaching freight train, and just in time I hugged the mast as *Cestus* rose and almost rolled over with the force of the wave. I crawled back into the cabin. Despite the heat of the night, I was in a cold sweat.

Below, I kept a deadly vigil with wet gear sloshing on the floorboards. The hull worked and groaned like rending wood. How much could I take before going out there again? How much pounding could *Cestus* take? Would the suspected crack split open and sink us? Bouncing around in the cabin, I realized this was probably my most terrifying ocean experience.

After I banged around inside the cabin for two hours, the wind and seas forced me to climb back on deck, this time without the harness, to triple reef the main. The gale was still building but I managed to stay aboard as the seas tried to shake me loose. Despite the limited visibility, I could see the foam of the breaking seas all around us. Down came the reefed jib in exchange for the storm jib. As I stepped down from the deck to the cockpit, a wave swamped the cockpit and I clutched the cabin door cover to save myself. Finally I was in the safety of the dank cabin.

I could hear waves advancing through the darkness and I prayed they would pass under me and not break on *Cestus*, which felt like an eggshell every time they hit.

I was already exhausted and the storm still raged. The top of my head was raw. The wind was roaring at about 45 knots, and the cabin was hideously damp. Bracing myself, I was determined to ride out the gale. But soon my muscles were weary from steadying myself in the heaving cabin. This gale is the equal of anything I experienced on my Hawaii, Tahiti or Japan voyages. I thought this could never happen this far north of Cape Horn, thousands of miles short of our goal.

Gale or no gale, I desperately needed rest. I jammed myself into my soggy bunk. The wind howled as I plunged into oblivion, only to emerge on the crest of a wave. Then the hull hurtled through space and pounded with the thudding voice of ruin.

For another two hours, I wondered how much longer we could take the brutal beating. From down below I knew we were in mortal danger. I had no choice. I had to go on deck again.

Going topside, I found not all was lost. I felt *Cestus* handling everything well. It proved amazingly seaworthy. The self-steering was working and we were actually making progress, despite a gale that seemed never to subside.

I went below and managed an uneasy sleep, ready to rise and save myself at a second's notice. We raced through the night out of control.

Racing The Ice To Cape Horn -- *By Frank Guernsey & Cy Zoerner*

Chapter Five

Springing A Leak
Before Crossing The Line

Mrs. Sullivan's Boarding School was another land of the giants where life was harsh and crossing the street was forbidden. If I could cross the street, I might be able to find my home. But I understood there were two homes now, that my beautiful mother and my father no longer lived together. It was confusing. Because they came for me on alternating weekends, a special disjointed relationship grew between us.

Mrs. Sullivan's school was a big house with ten boys and

girls as inmates. Assisted by a 300-pounder named Bernice, Mrs. Sullivan suffered no nonsense. Discipline was strict, and when we didn't learn our lessons, she literally grabbed offenders and banged our foreheads together. That helpless battering fostered a hatred for authority that would attend the rest of my days.

Our time was regimented. We rose at the same time, brushed our teeth at the same time, had breakfast at the same time, had our classes, lunch, more classes, play, dinner, study, and bedtime, all at the same time. It was all we knew and, in that sense, we had normal lives.

As much as anything else, resentment of this authority led me to sail alone. I wanted to be free.

The grades crept by, the deadly routine continued, broken by Tom Mix movies with my father some weekends. Mrs. Sullivan was giving us a solid, basic education. I was in fourth grade before I was at last permitted to cross the street and walk two miles alone to my mother's apartment. How I relished the adventure and the brief freedom.

Then in fifth grade, life became even more rigid. My father appeared in the door of our classroom during geography class, my favorite subject then because it released dreams of the wide world.

Mrs. Sullivan gave the class one of her classic stern looks and joined my father outside the door. My friend Monty shot a spitball at me with a forbidden rubber band -- how did he snitch it? -- but before I could react, the door opened and Mrs. Sullivan motioned to me. My father took my hand in a firm grasp.

"You're leaving Mrs. Sullivan, Frank. You're going to Cheviot Hills Military Academy."

"Isn't that exciting, Frank? Make us proud of you," Mrs. Sullivan said.

From the womb to the barracks, from short pants to a stiff uniform, all in one afternoon.

* * * * * * * * *

Time and again that night, we had run out of control. The gale and the crashing seas had pounded us for almost 48 hours. We took off from the tops of waves, soaring almost out of the water and crashing into the next roller. Even with all sails down, the rig shuttered from the sickening thrashing. This was terrifying! When the seas regained their sanity, we had gained about 1,500 miles toward Cape Horn, but *Cestus* was leaking.

Below, water glistened and sloshed around the floorboards. This was no longer the trickle I had spotted before the gale. At one time, I pumped 13 gallons from the bilge without a clue as to how it was getting in. The leak in the forward hatch couldn't account for that much. If the flooding didn't stop, I'd have to dive under the boat, and that was a dreadful prospect.

Before going overboard, I tried to remember how we had prepared *Cestus* to survive the savage oceans. Perhaps there was some clue to the leak. The first thing that came to mind was through-hull fittings, actual holes in the hull, capped with valves and used as drains. *Cestus* had five through-hull holes, three of them capped -- the two for the head and one at the sink drain. The remaining two were for the cockpit drains. It seemed unlikely that any of these fittings accounted for the leak.

It eventually dawned on me that the amount of sea water leaking into the hull matched sea conditions. In heavy seas, *Cestus* leaked alarmingly, in gentle seas hardly at all. Daily I was growing more convinced that there was only one explanation left: The joint between the hull and the deck was separating and, under stress, admitting water.

Cestus was built as many small sailboats are. One fiberglass shell was molded for the hull and another for the topsides. Including the deck, gunwales, cabin top, and cockpit, the topside shell is riveted -- and in less-expensive boats stapled

-- and glued to the hull shell.

The terrible toll the seas were taking on *Cestus*, combined with its venerable age, probably destroyed whatever had been caulking the seam. I'd add pumping the bilge to my daily routine.

At the moment, however, drinking water posed a more frightening problem than the leak. After the gales, my water bottles registered only two quarts. Time to try producing fresh water. Basically simple, the watermaker was still the most complex equipment aboard, except for the hand-held GPS and VHF radio.

The actual operation, however, was elementary. It was a pump with two hoses. One hose fit into a bucket of freshly scooped sea water, the other into a clean, empty bucket. Theoretically, 500 to 800 pumps on the handle provided freshwater for the day by forcing the saltwater through filters. However, I still wasn't sure how to change the filters.

I pumped until the muscles in my arms burned, but the watermaker produced only a sick dribble to dampen the bottom of the bucket. A terrible thirst descended on me and I was tempted to drink from the last of the bottled water.

"Though my life depends on this water pump, so far I can make only about three cups a day, far short of survival." I wrote in my sea diary. "So far the watermaker demands maximum effort for minimum output."

I thought about trying to salvage the steam from my tea. I did not realize the watermaker would simply take more effort.

In rough seas, I'd be forced to filter water inside the cabin, and doubtless both buckets would slosh over and make estimating the progress of the leak difficult.

 Storm systems flashed all around us. A small land bird, some kind of tropical species, flew in and landed exhausted on the aft deck. My best estimate put him almost 2,000 miles from Central America. Did the gales drive him, a feather in the blast, or did he hop from vessel to vessel? *Cestus* and I were delighted that he chose to share our fortune, providing me the opportunity to talk to another creature rather than to my video camera and *Cestus*. He soon got used to me and gained his sea legs. Though I coaxed him to eat and drink, he refused, and now interested large sea birds circled the boat. His chances seemed no better than mine.

Another gale struck and the tiny bird was lost. Over and over, *Cestus* leaped out of the water, and the following crash was like falling on concrete. The sea beat us for the rest of the night, shaking the foundation of the boat.

As we approached the equator, the satanic counter-currents tried to halt us in our tracks, but we staggered on. The counter-currents in this part of the Pacific seemed stronger than they had when I crossed the line on the way to Tahiti. The wind was right on our nose, and I estimated we were still 600 miles above the equator. That would mean 900 miles of sailing to the line because we couldn't sail directly into the south wind, and the waves were coming from the direction I was trying to sail. The best we could do was southeast to east, toward the coast of northern South America. Among the expressions sailors use to describe this point of sailing, "beating" and "going uphill" are probably best. Constant zigzagging against the winds and seas slows progress and builds enormous pressure on a fatigued sailor and his boat.

The wind alternated between squalls and flat calm with all the sails flopping. The self-steering gear needed six knots of wind to work, and during the calms I sat at the tiller eking out as much distance as possible. A cut on my finger, right at the bend, kept cracking open and stinging. During the night, the wind occasionally reached 60 knots, a nightmare howling outside the fiberglass shell.

As the weather alternated, now including rainstorms, I looked forward to opening the MREs -- meals ready to eat, much like the old military C-rations. According to my plan, I would start eating these super C-rations after crossing the equator. There were 113 MREs aboard, along with 75 Top Ramen for soup and plenty of cereal and powdered milk. In the meantime, my fresh food was running out. I especially missed grapefruit.

Partly because of the rough, non-skid surfaces on which I sat and partly because of my diet, my skin rash bled. Self-medication delivered no relief.

A routine guided my days: Brush teeth, straighten up the boat. Tang and vitamins. Pump the bilge. Wash my body. Take latitude and longitude with the GPS to find my position, later to be backed up by sextant, and plot it on my charts. Cereal, followed by a day's work and repair. Make drinking water, at least 45 minutes of exercise for the upper body. Shower, read the Bible, rest, eat an apple, read, rest, then blessed sunset cocktail hour, and dinner.

The hard work of constant reefing, unreefing, and changing of sails often interrupted my daily rituals.

Twenty-five days from Catalina with 75 more for Cape Horn -- if we could keep our grueling schedule. I was using a quart and a half of water a day for drinking and washing, now costing 800 strokes. But the watermaker functioned well.

My food stores continued to dwindle. My fresh coffee ran out, forcing cocoa as a replacement, until I began opening my MREs, which contained both coffee and cocoa. I put the last clean T-shirt on my sunburned body.

Fatigue forced me into dumb mistakes. One morning I lost a bucket overboard, a small item, but everything aboard is valuable. Then later a hat blew away. In the punishing equatorial sun, a hat is survival gear. In addition to my rash, I was managing to inflict cuts all over my body, not really knowing how.

As we approached the equator through confused seas, the heat was a pressure cooker. For nine days we seemed stuck to the water. On October 21, I made only 18 miles south. The icebergs were advancing at the bottom of the world, definitively winning our race, while we tried to struggle up a down escalator.

Sailing into the currents tortured the boat into incessant

groans. It sounded as if the aft hull structure were pulling apart. The supports we installed were feeling the pressure and trying to separate from the hull. The sound unnerved me, and bizarre dreams beset me in the churning darkness, as they often can alone at sea.

This wasn't to be the first time I crossed the equator. My first crossing was on the way to Tahiti over nine years ago. This time we would cross during the night without the heady thrill and special celebration. The beauty of crossing the line would be escaping the equatorial counter-currents. According to my charts, south of the equator, the seas would be less a cauldron and more steady currents from east to west unlike the Mentor current which can suck boat speed like quicksand.

I'd soon know if my MREs were spoiled from the sea conditions. If this happened, I would starve like a single-hander I remembered reading about. On his way from the Azores to the Virgin Islands, he starved aboard his small craft. When found, he was skeletal. I shuddered. Today had seen the end of my cocoa, cabbage, and desserts. I was as vulnerable as my food stores were finite. In terms of ultimate survival, provisioning was as crucial as rebuilding the boat for this ordeal.

Racing The Ice To Cape Horn -- *By Frank Guernsey & Cy Zoerner*

Chapter Six

Countering The
Counter-Currents

During the strangely cool night of October 23, we crossed the equator at about 116^0 West longitude. The next morning, I calculated that roughly averaging 3.8 sea miles per hour for the first 31 days, *Cestus* had eaten 35 percent of the distance to Cape Horn in 31 percent of my scheduled time.

The currents were to be more favorable by this time. The way we continued to buck and pound made me wonder where they were hiding. Examining the prevailing surface currents chart for summer (December, January, February), I saw the current streaming from east to west in our present position. But this was not what I encountered. *Cestus* continued to punch through the hellish chop that already had slowed us for days. The chart showed arrows that looked like whirlpools side by side and spinning in opposite directions north of the equator, not south where we were. Not that I expected one current to stop and another abruptly start. This was late October and maybe there was a big difference between the currents we now fought and the pattern five or six weeks later. Perhaps the summer charts didn't reflect the present conditions.

These seas threatened my timetable, and anything that threatened my timetable threatened my life.

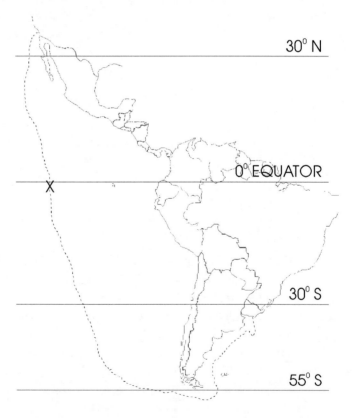

We had covered about 2,000 miles, and I estimated we still had more than 5,000 tough sea miles to Cape Horn.

Still blocking our path were these counter-currents, plus the Mentor current, in which the wind can go on extended vacations, gales and storms, lumbering iceberg mountains, and madness stalking us as surely as the ice.

Several hundred miles from the nearest point of land, south of the equator, I enjoyed my last orange. It was time to start eating my MREs. The 113 packets would be my staple for the rest of the voyage.

This would be my first experience with MREs. I probably should have tried one ashore, but they were relatively expensive. During my stint in the Marine Corps, we ate C-rations in the field. They weren't exactly "adventures in good eating," and I smiled when I thought of the gourmand who wrote a book by that name, Duncan Hines.

After fetching an MRE from the sopping locker, I checked out the dark-brown, plastic packet, measuring about a foot by eight inches. Big black letters announced:

SPAGHETTI WITH MEAT AND SAUCE
RIGHT AWAY FOODS
McALLEN, TEXAS 78501

Large 5's indicated that this was the fifth of the wide variety of MREs available.

The plastic package put up terrific resistance as I tried to tear and then bite it open. This was a sturdy container, and I hoped that it preserved the spaghetti well because my mouth was already watering. I finally sliced the bag open with my sharp little modified Bowie knife, veteran of all my voyages.

The first item to pop out was curious indeed. It was a flat, plastic packet a little over a foot long and about six inches wide. There was no question about its edibility. Covered with small print concerning warnings, operating instructions, and admonitions not to overfill, it was labeled MRE (Meal, Ready-to-Eat) Heater.

Ingenious. Fit the main course inside, pour water into the pouch, and the chemical heater was on the way to producing a hot meal in 15 minutes without a flame. It warned, however: "Vapors released by activated heater contain hydrogen, a flammable gas. Do not place an open flame in the vapor."

I decided to use my propane stove instead.

The spaghetti was in a flat, cardboard box that soon produced a brown plastic packet about nine inches long, important because of the size of my saucepan. I went below and put on a pan of saltwater to boil. Cooking was always a compromise. Using saltwater saved effort at the watermaker, but fresh water boils more quickly, saving propane. A boat is a self-contained system, full of interrelated compromises.

Then I inspected the rest of the All-American meal. Wrapped in heavy, brown plastic packages were crackers from Texas, cheese spread from Stone Mountain, Georgia, pound cake ("water activity stabilized") from San Antonio, a package of plain M&Ms from New Jersey, a packet of Cocoa Beverage Powder, Type 1, Fortified, from Kansas City, a one-serving envelope of Taster's Choice instant coffee and 6 grams of Domino sugar from New York, a cream substitute from Alabama, iodized salt from Georgia, a Refreshing Towelette from Connecticut, a light-green pack of damp-weather paper matches from North Carolina, and a tiny bottle of Tabasco sauce from New York, followed by a pack of toilet paper from San Francisco. The two green squares of chewing gum, a sugar-free iced tea drink mix, and a brown plastic spoon claimed no origin. The sturdy spoon could, no doubt, dig foxholes.

Unlike the C-rations of old, there were no cigarettes.

The water had begun to boil, but I discovered that the stiff, plastic pack of precooked spaghetti did not fit into my pan easily. Nonetheless, in ten minutes I was keeping my balance while cutting open the spaghetti packet. A few minutes later, a tangy smell accompanied my attack on the main course. It was delicious, not exactly from Mama Marie's, but proper fare for an offshore sailor. I wished there were more spaghetti. Squeezing the cheese package over the hearty pair of crackers produced a smooth sheet that required little spreading with my spoon. A good first MRE meal.

After feasting on the hot spaghetti, I considered my course. It was simply to keep Easter Island to port, turn for Cape Horn, skirt the icebergs and hope. I wrote in my log:

"Interesting to read the pilots and see that there are gales near cape horn more than 50% of the time in December. Everything I've been reading about the cape is more than ominous. It's a strange feeling to want to live but to be with each day perhaps running toward my death with each day to become more torturous until it becomes unbearably miserable and cold and no one will know how far I got or if I quit. To hell with it. I intend to live, miracle or no."

Then I resumed eating my pound cake, too sweet for my taste, but doubtless packed with energy. I washed down my meal with a half-cup of my precious drinking water, produced now by 1,000 strokes per day.

Desalinated water isn't designer water, but it is pure and refreshing. Thank God for the PUR corporation; the watermaker was the most valuable piece of equipment aboard.

To see what flavor the chewing gum was, I tried it -- wintergreen -- but I spit it out immediately because who wants cavities at sea? Even so, I'd pop the M&Ms for the rest of the day.

Rummaging below, I found one of my large yard leaf bags brought along for trash. I don't mind tossing biodegradable trash overboard, or anything the fish or birds will eat. But plastic violates the ocean and its creatures in the most violent way, and plastic foam in particular takes hundreds of years to deteriorate.

Almost all the packaging in the MREs was plastic, and I didn't want to litter the ocean or choke unsuspecting sea creatures. After finishing my meal with a sense of well-being, I gazed at the slow lurch of the water and shut my eyes, feeling the sun on my face.

* * * * * * * * * *

"I can't go to military school in short pants," I pleaded. Knowing there would be big boys strutting around in military uniforms, I was close to tears of humiliation. "The big boys will laugh at me."

"Don't be silly, Frank. We don't have time for you to change. We've an appointment with the commander at 11 o'clock. Get hold of yourself," my father admonished.

"Please."

"You're too old for Mrs. Sullivan's school now, and Cheviot Hills will make a man out of you. You want to be a man, don't you?"

"I guess so."

Cheviot Hills Military Academy boasted a sprawling campus, though complex or compound might be more accurate words. It could have been called a fort. But even as a ten-year-old, I could see it for what it was -- a new form of confinement.

The commander was in full military uniform, bright ribbons over the left pocket of his olive-drab jacket. He sat with his back to a large window overlooking the playing fields, a menacing silhouette topped by a halo of silver hair.

He folded his hands on the gleaming desktop near a single manila folder. Explaining the fine traditions of Cheviot Hills Military Academy, he emphasized that I'd be expected to uphold them. I'd be taught obedience and teamwork, and provided the foundation for a good, moral character.

"That's excellent, Colonel," my father said.

I'd be placed in one of the ten Indian tribes that formed the structure of the academy. I'd eat, sleep, play, study, and live with my tribe. He opened the file folder and, with hardly a downward glance, said, "You'll be a Mohican. Some good men in that tribe."

Though he was talking to me, he looked at father. I got

the impression that the colonel was putting on a show for my father, who smiled and nodded through much of the interview.

"We'll take good care of young Frank here, sir," the commander said to my father.

"I'm sure you will." The two men rose and shook hands. The pact was sealed.

As soon as my father left, the man would beat me, I was sure. Luckily, I was wrong. The commander, like much of the cadre, was stern and aloof, but not at all sadistic.

Instead, he said, "Now, Cadet Guernsey, follow me to the quartermaster's. We'll get you out of those short pants and into uniform."

I blushed, and said, "Yes, sir," according to the rules he had outlined.

Although I was almost running to keep up with his long strides, I noticed uniformed boys in the polished hallways. None of them showed more than curiosity, and there were no catcalls about my exposed knees. In fact, they stood at silent attention as we passed. Some of them wore yellow stripes on their sleeves.

We entered a room without windows, and the commander said, "Mohican," and turned me over to a younger officer with reading glasses perched on the end of his nose. He scrutinized me for a few awkward moments and then went to the shelves of folded, olive-drab uniforms. Swiftly, he picked out several.

"They'll fit," the commander said. "Now follow me."

He had to remind me to respond "yes, sir." Again I trotted behind him through the polished hall. Upstairs, we entered a large room, sterile, looking and smelling like a hospital. I put on my uniform and sat alone on my bunk. A gold stripe ran down the trousers, the jacket was unadorned by military insignia or stripes, the khaki shirt with bow tie was tight around my neck.

After the last class, cadets filed quietly into the barracks. I identified myself as a Mohican, and immediately a small group of boys gathered around me and explained that the Mohicans had to be the best tribe, a perfect tribe, and I would have to do everything possible to contribute to that.

Through an elaborate system, the faculty and administrators awarded points for behavior, discipline, academics, patriotism, sports, and other endeavors to each cadet. The points were assigned to his tribe, and the tribe with the highest total was declared best. This was my first taste of peer pressure as a control mechanism.

That night after taps, I lay wide awake in my bunk. At the end of the large room, an "officer of the day" sat at a small wooden table reading by a goose-necked lamp.

The path to survival was clear. Conform. If you conform, you will be OK, or at least avoid punishment. Deviate, and life will fall on you like an avalanche. The colonel had made that clear.

There in the semi-dark barracks, I decided to become an invisible puppet, do whatever I was told, become a good cadet, help the Mohicans as much as possible, call no undue attention to myself. Years later in Japan, I heard an expression that summarized my strategy: "The nail that sticks up highest is the first to be hit on the head."

In the days that followed, my confidence grew. I was not the youngest boy at CHMA, which ran from preschool to ninth grade.

My fellow cadets were mostly rich kids. I was lucky because I began spending alternate weekends with my parents. Some of the other boys lived in the academy year round and seldom saw their parents, many of whom resided in Europe. Once a year, mother took me to the circus. She must have known how much that would mean to me. How proud I was to be seen with this beautiful woman, knowing she was my mother, and feeling that every other kid under the big top was envious.

About this time, a man entered her life. In my mind, he will always remain "R.L." He ran the powerful *Los Angeles Daily News*.

Academically, I had an advantage, and this further boosted my confidence. Mrs. Sullivan had given me a solid background, and I responded to the academy's excellent faculty.

My conformity was indeed rewarded. Never was I forced to kneel in front of the class, a common punishment. My straight A's elevated the Mohicans, and I would finish the year *summa cum laude*. In the parades we staged for the parents, I held a place of honor as bearer of the American flag. Definitely, I felt, there was a place for me at Cheviot Hills Military Academy.

* * * * * * * * * *

When I opened my eyes again, we were making about a half-knot. Though I had spent years planning and securing my provisions, I began worrying. Would I have enough to last until the end of the voyage? My earlier ocean crossings provided good guidelines. The basic trick is stuffing enough food, water, and equipment to sustain life at sea into the extremely limited space of a small sailboat.

Already the sea reminded me of the important things I had overlooked as I prepared for the voyage. Some kind of slippers to wear inside the boat for comfort and warmth. Night binoculars to keep watch and avoid collisions in the dangerous shipping lanes. More T-shirts. A corkscrew, thin towels, cups, extra buckets, more toothpaste. All of this would have made life more comfortable.

My diet now consisted mainly of MREs, soup, beans, rice, cold cereal, powdered milk, Tang, tuna, Spam, garlic, honey, sardines, powdered eggs, dried fruit, jerky, cookies, anchovies, canned meats, crackers, and other canned and packaged treats. Daily doses of multiple vitamins and vitamin C held this all together.

The most important addition to my minimal medical kit was Imodium, a remedy for diarrhea. The second most important medical item was one quart of Jack Daniel's and one quart of Wild Turkey, though they were at risk for recreational purposes.

My spirits locker contained five gallons of brandy and one bottle of wine reserved for Thanksgiving. I always drink in moderation. Drunkenness would put me into stupid jeopardy.

My ship's library of 24 books provided food and drink for the mind. In addition to the Bible, I loved the *Book of Friends*, the last gasp of Henry Miller, an author I enjoy. Classic sea stories, classic novels, along with a Mickey Spillane and some philosophy, completed my library.

A friend gave me a volume of condensed books, loaded with fearsome tales of the sea. Just when I needed encouragement, I was reading *Boon Island,* the true story of a shipwrecked crew on an island within sight of the lights of an Eastern city. The castaways on Boon Island slowly starved while watching the tantalizing lights by night.

Another of the condensations was the story of men trapped for weeks in a life raft. Slowly they died of starvation while encircled by blood-thirsty sharks. Hardly cheery fare for a lone voyager, but I couldn't stop turning the pages.

The next two weeks, we struggled against the currents and counter-currents. The waves and current -- not the wind -- continued to hammer *Cestus*. It was like being in a washing machine, going nowhere fast. How we longed for the rhythm of following seas to push us along.

The last of the potatoes rotted with damp, and everything aboard, including the skipper, remained soggy. The camera, film, and video recorder were wet. On one leg alone, I counted twenty saltwater sores. If there were a dry square inch aboard, I couldn't find it. *Cestus* was a pneumonia pit.

Disturbing dreams plagued me by night, especially dreams of my mother, and by day I obsessed about the Good Samaritan who demanded scotch as his due. Waging a battle against bad thoughts, I entered in my sea diary that unless my attitude became more positive, I could lose it out here.

But by 1 p.m. that day, the sea eased my mind. We

gamboled along in the finest sailing day to date. A wind of about 13 knots blew from our starboard beam. For the joy of it, I disengaged Leo, the self-steering device, and took the helm. *Cestus* felt perfectly balanced, the tiller a feather in my left hand, as the reefed mainsail and working jib drew us happily toward our goal.

The ship was alive and, after all these thousands of miles, the excitement of splendid sailing again gripped me.

Cestus shook aside spray like a wet dog and the drops glistened in tropical sun, frozen in midair before falling into the trail of bubbles that marked our swift progress. Surely at the moment we were winning the race with the icebergs.

The wind swept through my lengthening hair and around my ears, whispering a sea song, urging us on, making us wish this moment would last for eternity. This ancient song of the sea mingled with the whooshing spray and the sounds of an ecstatic sailboat. No moaning now, just movement and joy.

Our speed cooled me in air that smelled so pure that it might have whisked all the way from Australia.

Another two weeks, with luck, would find us halfway to the Cape.

But as I was preparing for cocktail hour and sunset, the good weather fled like a weakling from a challenge, and by midnight the large, confused seas battered us from all directions.

The compass sheered its plastic mount and from then on I'd be forced to hold it in my hand. We slowed to under two knots -- a child could toddle faster, it seemed -- and later my calculations showed we made only 60 sea miles that day.

The wind and seas continued to confound me.

Sleepless nights of reliving the mercurial relationship with Mary followed days in which zero wind suddenly soared to blasts beyond my experience, knocking *Cestus* on beam's end like a bathtub toy. At other times, the string of audio tape tied to the shrouds as a telltale for the wind would wrap lackadaisically around the wire.

As the mast etched lazy zigzags across the dark sky, an

alarming amount of sea water sloshed below, renewing my worry about the leak. After pumping 16 gallons from the bilge at one time, I feverishly tore through the hold searching for a crack but could find none. Without a fiberglass liner, *Cestus* bared her raw hull, and if there were cracks they should have been visible.

I tried my short-wave radio receiver, but only China came through.

We passed far to the west of Ecuador, then Peru. The elusive leak swamped the lockers below, and I struggled to keep a water watch around the clock.

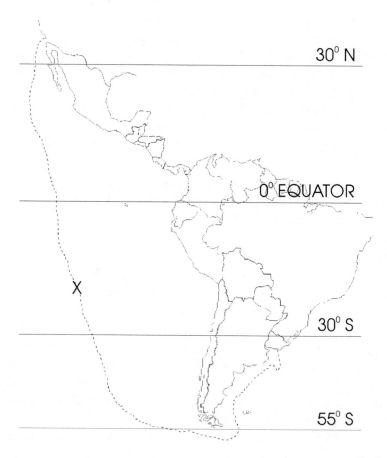

A scheduled eclipse of the sun eluded me entirely. But reflection on the clockwork of the universe reminded me that no matter how we value our independence and self-reliance, a higher power makes or breaks events. No way would I make it around the Cape without the help of that higher power.

New obstacles lay ahead. Thoughts of sailing into the shipping lanes distressed me. I could see the sharp, cleaving bow of a freighter towering over the stern. A deep fatigue set in, making me clumsy. I lost a pair of trunks overboard. I was putting things away in the wrong place, repeating myself in the sea diaries, and the icebergs loomed huge, cold, and hard in my imagination.

Despite all of this, my spirits always recovered at sunset. The western sky was lowering and a strange yellow sun slowly deepened to gold. The dark clouds caught fire and the chopping water to the west smoldered like a vast pot of shining, copper pennies.

On election day, November 8, *Cestus* fought for our lives, the mainsail triple-reefed and water flooding the cockpit. The seas stumbled over themselves and swamped the cockpit.

I was below bailing when a wave broke with doomsday force and rolled us over with me cramped in the tiny forward locker of the boat. I don't know how, but *Cestus* righted and went about its business. I began to wonder if we'd ever make it to the Tropic of Capricorn, according to my figures only two sailing days south.

Exhausted, I wedged myself into my drenched bunk and fell into that twilight between deep sleep and wakefulness. In my semi-comatose state, I felt each pitch, yaw, and roll as *Cestus* shouldered its way through the currents. The dank cabin dripped condensation onto my bunk, wind whined outside. I decided that sailing on the edge must stop. Despite the shortened sail, *Cestus* bent far to lee. At last I fell into a deep sleep.

Catapulted from my bunk, I awoke suspended near the ceiling as the boat rolled to the rail and white pain flashed in my skull as my elbow smashed into fiberglass hull.

Chapter Seven

Grasping At The Wind

The summer after my first year at Cheviot Hills Military Academy was paradise. I lived with my Uncle Luke, Aunt Bobby, and my three cousins, Di (short for Darius), Denny, and Karen. For the first time, I was living within a family. In September, I'd be a sixth-grader.

After World War II, Luke, my father's brother, married Bobby, my mother's friend. They made the San Fernando Valley their home, moving to Sherman Oaks, at the foot of the Sepulveda Pass north of west Los Angeles.

In those days, the valley was still cowboy country, hot

and dry, with a rural flavor, though tract houses were sprouting as fast as developers could build them to meet the demand of returning GIs, armed with loans provided by their grateful country.

In the evening, we gathered around the radio, like most American families in those post-war years. I was struck by the report of the newly launched *United States* setting a record on her maiden transatlantic voyage.

Sometimes, when there was a lull in the programming, Uncle Luke, his hazel eyes taking on a far-away look, would weave adventure stories about his life as a major in the Army

The house, which sat across from walnut and plum orchards, was an idyllic location for children. My cousins were built-in playmates, and the neighborhood children were boisterous companions. Not one of them wore a uniform, saluted, or marched in close-order drill.

We had just the right amount of supervision -- freedom to be kids, but protection from chaos. Aunt Bobby was one of the kindest women I have ever known. She was warm and nurturing, and though her house was neat and clean, it was comfortable. The difference between Aunt Bobby's and the Academy was the difference between velvet and steel.

The smell of her bread baking in the kitchen made my mouth water. The food at Mrs. Sullivan's and at Cheviot Hills was nutritious and plentiful, but it was institutional. Aunt Bobby cooked with a loving hand, and I could taste the difference.

"You know what we do, Frank?" Di said shortly after I arrived. His tone hinted of conspiracy against all adults. "We have rock fights!"

"And you know what else?" His voice was heavy with the deliciously forbidden.

It was hard to think of anything more enjoyable.

"Come with us."

My cousins sped through the house, emerging with bows and arrows from their most sacred hiding places. We tore through the neighborhood and kids joined our swarm like bees, each armed with bows and plenty of arrows.

Led by Di, we raced across the little-traveled road and into the vast, taboo orchard. I was excited by the wild plunge and the daring idea that whatever happened, adults would surely disapprove.

We stopped under a canopy of walnut trees, the teal blue sky peeking down. Di equipped me with his extra bow and arrow.

"Ready?" he called. The kids slotted their arrows, and pointed their bows upward. I followed suit.

"Aim," Di commanded. The kids drew back the strings mightily. This was my first experience with a weapon.

"Fire."

The arrows shot up through the branches and the squealing kids ran helter-skelter. I stood dumbfounded.

"Run, Frank," Di yelled enthusiastically. "You'll be killed by an arrow."

The summer slipped away in all manner of kids' delight. Only in late August, when the valley sizzled and we often had vanilla ice cream with dinner, did I begin dreading my return to Cheviot Hills, the disinfected barracks, the Mohicans, the rules.

At least, I was returning to a known environment, a familiar routine. I wouldn't be the new boy. I liked some of the other cadets, and my place was clear and secure -- part of the Mohican tribe. And I was a top-rated student.

On the dreaded day my father came to return me to the academy, he bore the news that Cheviot Hills had gone out of business during the summer. I would enter the prestigious California Military Academy.

* * * * * * * * * *

After the seas hurled me from my bunk, I regained control, and again we survived the vicious seas. Though I favored my elbow for a few days, nothing was broken. South of the Tropic of Capricorn, the air grew cooler and I converted from a blanket to my mummy sleeping bag. My Antarctic bag would come later.

Intermittent squalls drenched us, and I could see them scudding across the water, and then BAM!, they'd hit and sprint on. Between squalls, dead calms suspended time. While *Cestus* rocked impatiently, I would seethe in frustration.

On the fiftieth day, we were approaching Isla de Pascua, Easter Island, the last outpost. The maddening water in the cabin gurgled and swilled, but I decided not to dive under the boat, because what would I do if I found the trouble? I'd sail toward the Horn till we sank, I vowed.

Dejectedly, I studied the pilot charts, squinting at the intermittent red line of icebergs. Just before noon, a large flying fish landed on the deck, my only catch of the voyage. Though I had planned to supplement my diet with ocean fish, I had no luck. The self-steering gear hung so far over the stern it probably would have prevented landing a fish anyway. Little six-inch fish had surfed in the bow wave for several weeks. My fatigue had convinced me that the same fish were accompanying us.

The very next day, I decided to dive under the boat. I pulled on trunks, tied a line around my chest and secured it to *Cestus*. I disconnected Leo and lowered the sails to prevent the boat from sailing away, dragging me behind it like a hooked fish. I waited for perfect conditions.

Finally, a dead calm. Deep blue, bottomless water. Little fish following the boat. On with my cheap goggles.

I was terrified.

Would I have the strength to heave myself back aboard?

Splashing into the warm water, I entered an alien world. I searched the clear water fearfully for sharks. As best I could, I inspected the hull, bobbing up for air as I went. I surveyed the port side, then starboard. The hull appeared seamless. I was going down again to inspect the rudder when, suddenly, two torpedoes streaked toward me.

Sharks!

About six feet long. Lethal teeth flashing. I scrambled to grab a shroud to pull myself aboard. I could feel my feet sliced off. With all my might, I heaved out of the water and aboard *Cestus*. I was aboard, safe, intact.

The two made one more pass. From the safety of the cockpit, I realized they weren't sharks, probably not even predators. Wahoos, perhaps. In my primitive terror, anything dark, big, and fast was a shark.

Days passed in calms. As my anxiety about the leak diminished, my anxiety about our schedule increased. At worst, the leak was probably the seam between the deck and hull, but falling behind schedule could be lethal. Often I took down the sails to avoid the annoying flapping as the boat rocked. I worried that the snapping could tear the seams, despite Ed Taylor's good work.

There was torment in my voice as I repeatedly complained to the video recorder, "We're going up and down more than forward." Though estimating we were halfway to Cape Stiff, I could imagine we were hovering over the same spot on the bottom, thousands of feet below. "And when we can tack, we're just sailing east and west, back and forth, rather than making headway for the Cape."

The red, pimply rash flared again. Curious about how it looked and optimistic that one day I'd see my tapes, I videotaped my backside, a hideous sight. A change of diet in the Marine Corps had produced a similar rash. Perhaps my new daily fare was to blame.

As we rocked in hypnotic rhythm, I dug through the MREs in the bilge, looking for the leak. Finding the only turkey meal left aboard, I decided to save it for Thanksgiving dinner, about eleven days away. That day, I'd drink the wine Cousin Denny and his wife, Jan, had given me.

Our position was now about 28^0 South latitude, and most of that Sunday we were prisoners of a calm. As the countdown clock ticked, sailing became a nightmare of immobility.

How quickly the sea changes. Thirty-one hours later, the wind raced across the glassy water, in sight before I could feel its welcome breath. By late afternoon, we were rocketing along. I prayed it would hold.

But at 2 a.m., the snapping sails awakened me. I entreated the gods for wind once again. In the dark and quiet, my mind ranged over my enemies and obstacles. Probably the leak could have been prevented by caulking the hull-deck seam. My annoying benefactor at Avalon infected my head yet again. I dismissed him by centering on the joys of being offshore alone, adventuring on the ultimate run.

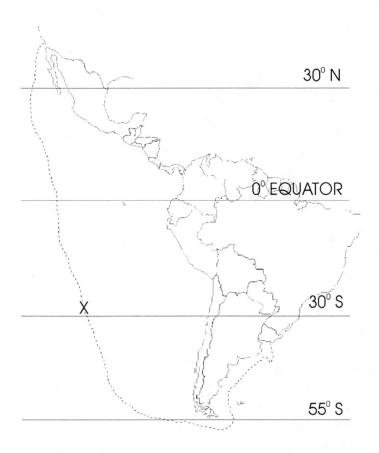

In the past two days, we had made about 120 miles. The icebergs were gaining on us, preparing a deadly rendezvous. I was distressed, yet equally excited.

Even as I grappled with the immediate future, I had time to look into the distant future. After an experience like this one, how could I ever be much of a life insurance prospector again?

My mind turned to Mary. I wished we were sitting in the sunshine on the beach near Santa Barbara.

With the jib up, in a gentle breeze, the next morning we turned for Cape Horn. It was day fifty-four and our location was approximately 30^0 South latitude, roughly 300 miles southwest of the silent megaliths on Easter Island and about 2,000 from the mainland at La Serena, Chile. Our longitude was 117^0 West, not far east from the line that runs through Los Angeles.

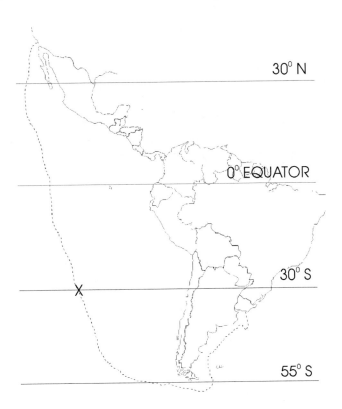

The turn thrilled me. Now we would bear directly toward the Cape. In light rain, we ghosted along in a whisper, following the 30th parallel. For the first time in weeks, we followed a starboard tack, resurrecting every creak of the hull. Nobody yet knew how long fiberglass lasts. Would I be the first to find out as age turned our hull into a brittle shell?

Changing a frayed line on the wind vane, I discovered the boat-store clerk had sold me a line slightly larger than required. It would chafe in the block and wear out quickly. The question was, how quickly?

We were stuck in a parking lot that covered approximately half of the earth. I reached out ahead with clawed fingers trying to grasp the air and pull us forward.

* * * * * * * * *

California Military Academy was Cheviot Hills in spades. It had more discipline, higher expectations, and elevated academic standards. Once again, conformity pointed the clear way to survival.

There were about 20 kids to a class. Here, too, were the rich, many from distinguished families, although our uniforms reduced the differences. Among my classmates were Nicky Charisse, son of dancer Cyd Charisse, and Cary Agajanian, whose father was the famed owner of Indianapolis race cars.

Cheviot Hills had taught me that I could distinguish myself. I could rise to the top of my class and perhaps be named Honor Cadet of the Year. In CMA's words, "The Academy established the Honor Cadet Award to stress the importance of three basic principles: military training to instill habits of promptness, obedience, and alertness; good conduct as the foundation of good citizenship; and thorough scholastic attainments for successful living."

That would be Cadet Guernsey: prompt, obedient, alert, a boy of good conduct and a scholastic attainer.

I also played all the sports the academy offered, and

found that I was good at football.

Each year, CMA joined with a prominent girls' school to stage a ball. In my early years, I wondered why the older boys were so keen on dancing when CMA offered football, baseball, basketball, and track.

Life changed in many ways while I was at CMA. My mother married R.L. and established a home in Bel Air, across from the golf course. In contrast, when my father remarried, providing me with a stepmother, Nancy, they moved to a tract house in the San Fernando Valley.

Alternating weekends between these homes was a study in lifestyles. Although R.L. was a high roller who lived like a sultan, he let me work at the golf course during my visits. One afternoon late in the fall with clouds threatening rain, I caddied for Clark Gable.

R.L.'s cronies were in and out of the Bel Air estate. One afternoon, I found R.L. in the study with a tall, thin, handsome man.

"This is Mr. Hughes," R.L. said, "...my stepson, Frank."

"Hello, Frank," he said.

Much later I realized this was Howard Hughes.

My father and Nancy offered a comfortable home in the Valley. While staying with them in eighth grade, I was withdrawn from CMA and placed in Birmingham Junior and Senior High School. The change was shocking. My new classmates were undisciplined. Many of them contended that learning was for "squares."

It was easy to fall in with the wrong crowd. They were most alluring, independent, rebellious, cigarette-smoking, cool. Marveling at the lack of discipline, I goofed off and my studies faltered. I grew restless and resentful.

I soon found myself back at CMA, but public school had sullied me. I was unable to regain my position as top student. I would never be Honor Cadet of the Year.

But fortunes have a way of changing, and when they did, I left CMA again. I moved in with my mother and R.L., who now lived in Park La Brea without a butler or a Bentley parked in the garage. I spent ninth grade at John Burroughs Junior High School, a sharp contrast to Birmingham. Burroughs was filled with high achievers. It was essentially the last year of my true education until I entered college ten years later.

Whether in private or public schools, summers found me in various camps. My favorite summers were spent at the Los Dos Pueblos Ranch, owned by a friend of R.L.'s, Sam Mosher. Owning the Flying Tigers freight line, Signal Oil, and other major interests made Mr. Mosher one of the richest men in the United States.

The vast ranch bordered on the Pacific Ocean. The center of activity was a baronial ranch house surrounded by the workers' cottages. Cattle grazed the land, and the ranch sported its own dairy and a zoo, consisting of bobcats, mountain lions, badgers, deer, and other animals captured on the grounds.

As one of the hands, I earned room and board and $75 per month helping with the 10-acre vegetable gardens. The work satisfied me with a new sense of reality. Once a week, we harvested the vegetables and delivered them to the cottages and the main ranch house. We ate what we grew, and the vegetables were delicious.

I worked long hours with another boy under the supervision of an old Scot, Sam Aiken, but at 5 p.m., I was absolutely, completely, definitely, truly, positively free for the first time in my life.

I was 14.

Pockets loaded with money, I'd hitchhike into Santa Barbara on Saturdays to indulge in orgies of burger eating, chocolate malt swilling, and candy chomping. Though tempted to stop into a liquor store for a six-pack, I was too embarrassed to try.

On the ranch lived Ila, a beautiful, dark-haired girl, budding with femininity. Her father was one of the permanent residents. I was smitten.

Because I was so awkward, Ila failed to notice my

passion. The end of summer and the unrequited love filled me with bittersweet emotion.

The anticipation of losing my brief freedom was like the tightening jaws of a vice, though life with my mother and R.L. was far from grim.

And it seemed that end of summer was always the time for bombshells. I wasn't disappointed. My father picked me up in his Oldsmobile and informed me that my mom had gone away and I would be living with him and Nancy in the Valley, where I'd attend Van Nuys High School. This was the end of life as I knew it.

Racing The Ice To Cape Horn -- *By Frank Guernsey & Cy Zoerner*

Chapter Eight

Ghosting Through The Mentor Current

If the counter-currents made me grasp for the wind, the Mentor current stretched my sanity. If walking on water were possible, I could have hiked to Cape Horn faster than at my present rate. In sheer frustration, I knelt in the cockpit and paddled with my hands, but the frigid water and my raw skin soon cured me of that folly. Making 30 miles in 24 hours seemed like a good day.

My chart labeled the current as "weak and variable,"

showing it generally rotating in a counterclockwise direction, but we were experiencing current from every direction, though mostly on our nose. There was no doubt we languished in the Mentor current.

Somehow, we must push through this region of anxiety into the Roaring Forties.

Now there was a chill in the air and my mummy bag and everything else aboard was clammy. I estimated we were 700 miles from the ice, but the Mentor current trapped us in its giant palm, and we seemed to be wandering around for weeks and ending up in the same spot.

With 43 days left on my countdown calendar, we made 30 miles west and 30 miles south for a total of 60 miles and a net gain of 0. The next day I took down the sails while we rocked rhythmically.

Then suddenly, at 2 a.m., we broke from the trap. I was out on deck as fast as possible to set sail, and we cooked toward Cape Horn. An hour later, we were out of control, and I crawled back on deck to reef.

All day, we roared along, a new creak probably indicating the cockpit's effort to break away from a support we glassed in.

We beat into tall, breaking seas for two straight days, and the seas beat us back. For man and ship, these were two full days of misery. I ran my hands over my beard and realized that the face beneath was sunken.

What would it be like south of 40^0, where the most severe tests were yet to come? Could my little boat really contend with worse conditions? Each storm and each pounding by heavy seas made me think *Cestus* had reached the limit of her endurance. But each time, almost unbelievably, *Cestus* plowed onward, taking everything the Pacific had to offer.

Had I really selected the right boat for this adventure, or would it come apart before reaching our goal?

* * * * * * * * * *

Selecting a boat for Cape Horn had been like selecting a marriage partner, except more serious. A mistake in selecting a spouse leads to painful times; a mistake in choosing a Cape Horner puts your good times on hold forever.

The Los Angeles megalopolis offers a confusing choice of sailing yachts. There are over 100 marinas, 68 yacht clubs, 119 yacht brokers (not to mention new boat dealers), and uncounted storage yards, all bristling with sailboats. Trailer boats to 25 feet crowd thousands of local driveways. About 1,400 boats reside in King Harbor, and eight sea miles north in Marina del Rey, another 6,500 fill one of the largest yacht harbors in the United States.

Where was my Cape Horner? The number of potential boats was mind-boggling.

The *Los Angeles Times*, the local *South Bay Daily Breeze*, and yachting publications such as *The Log* offer wonderful classified sections. There is also the sailor's eternal grapevine.

I had described my requirements to Ross Angel, a King Harbor live-aboard with solo voyaging aspirations of his own. Though eccentric, he was the most knowledgeable and enthusiastic small-boat sailor I knew.

Ross was in his 40s, graying, with the weathered skin of a sea dog. He was a member of the King Harbor Yacht Club, one of two in the harbor at the time. He raced Challengers and often won.

The notion of my Cape Horn venture excited his blood, and he volunteered to help me find a boat. I accepted gratefully.

"My number one consideration in looking for a boat is hull integrity," I explained. "The hull must be able to stand up to hellish seas. I need a hull that makes all my previous boats look flimsy.

"The second most important thing is money."

That didn't surprise Ross, who guessed my modest means. Given my prowess in the insurance business, $2,000 was my top dollar for a boat. Although I wouldn't buy a suspect boat because of the low price, I would have to pass up many sound hulls priced out of my range.

I didn't want to make the Cape Horn run in a boat shorter than 22 feet or longer than 40 feet. Ross asked for my ideal boat.

"It would be a 32-footer with a diesel engine. That size would seem palatial after the small boats I've sailed."

Along with size comes comfort, but also more maintenance. When you're in trouble, the bigger the boat, the bigger the trouble. Given my humble budget, however, I knew that my Cape Horner would probably likewise be of humble length.

"Also no boat with hard chines," I specified.

A hard-chined boat has relatively flat, almost vertical slab sides and a flatish or vee bottom. The ridges where the sides and bottom join are called the chines. A boat with hard chines initially resists capsizing, but once it does start to turn over, there's nothing stopping it.

Better for my purpose would be a boat with rounded sides and bottom with no ridge. Though such a round chine boat tips up quickly in a wind, it then grows stiff and more difficult to tip over. I figured it would give me a chance in the oceans surrounding Antarctica.

"Finally, no fin keels," I instructed.

A fin keel vaguely resembles an inverted shark's fin. My preference was a full keel, one running the length of the boat. A full keel, I believed, would cut a truer track in heavy seas and make steering easier.

I could overlook a number of details because I planned to replace, refurbish, and reinforce whatever the boat needed. Because of my successful voyages to Tahiti, Hawaii, and Japan, Ross respected my nautical judgment.

The long and frustrating search for a Cape Horner was

on. Either the boats were fundamentally weak and beyond beefing up, or they were impossibly expensive.

One gentle April day in 1991, Ross was driving north on the San Diego Freeway in Gardena, a few miles inland from Redondo Beach, when he spotted a boat in the Ace Storage yard. He pulled to the side of the roaring freeway, galloped down a bank of slippery ice plant and, much to the chagrin of the owner, climbed the chain-link fence to check out his find. There a Gladiator, a boat Ross highly respected, perched on a rusty yard trailer.

Ross saw the life that could be breathed into the venerable sloop, and rushed back to the marina.

Awakened from a nap aboard my borrowed boat, I heard and felt his rapid approach down the dock. "Frank," he called. "I've found a Gladiator!"

At the time, I probably wouldn't have recognized a Gladiator. Certainly, I knew nothing of their sailing history, nor had I ever sailed aboard one.

Nevertheless, his find piqued my curiosity. His enthusiasm infected me, and I headed for Gardena. The sky was blue and the air was clear after the previous day's showers. A perfect day to buy a Cape Horner.

I found the dilapidated little sloop hiding in a corner of the yard behind an old ice cream truck. The neglect was palpable. The California sunlight only accented its shabbiness. Its snapped mast gave it the crushed look of a bird with a broken wing. A most discouraging sight and a most unlikely candidate for a Cape Horner, at least at first glance.

Did I really want to marry this boat?

I ran my fingers over the hull and felt the stony chill of a cadaver. An empty shell, it was a dismal blue, part of the detritus that people forget in storage yards, paying the monthly fees by rote. Defunct cars, motor homes, and other keepsakes, sentimental junk no longer worth the fees, but too heavy in nostalgic value to sell or abandon.

Yet this forlorn specimen did meet my requirements.

The fiberglass hull seemed anvil solid. At 24 feet, it barely fell within my lower limit. It was 20 feet on the waterline. Waterline is important because its length determines the theoretical top speed of a sailboat, a consideration in my race with the icebergs.

The rounded hull met my soft-chine criterion, and the keel ran the length of the boat. The flat, uncluttered foredeck was a bonus, making for good footing as I changed headsails in pitching seas. The price of a flat deck was the low headroom inside the cabin, a price my bloody head would pay over and over.

By its looks, even I could afford this forlorn specimen.

Ross' voice resounded through my head: "Gladiators are sound little boats, Frank, just what you're looking for. They're a Bill Lapworth design, and you just can't beat him or his boats."

Later I learned from a mid-1960s promotional brochure that Gladiators are seven and a half feet wide. Displacing 3,850 pounds of water (the weight of the empty boat), they need a minimum of four feet of water to float. Their headroom inside the cabin is four feet, nine inches. New, their price was $4,450, relatively expensive for their time.

According to their manufacturer, Continental Plastics Corporation of Costa Mesa, California, they were intended for day sailing, racing, and modest cruising. Naval architects design daysailers for an afternoon in moderate winds and mild seas. The brochure called Lapworth "one of the world's finest Naval Architects," his creation "stiff, dry, and seaworthy regardless of weather."

Lapworth designed the boat with a fractional rig, meaning that the headsail does not reach to the top of the mast, a fraction of its height. Continental Plastics assured prospective buyers that it used "the finest materials available" in the construction of the daysailer.

This daysailer's name was *Cestus*, the name of the leather thongs Roman boxers bound to their fists in gladiatorial matches. There's a tradition among sailors that it's bad luck to rename a boat. Though I don't consider myself superstitious, I wouldn't rename my ship.

Besides, I liked the name. I had images of *Cestus* punching through the seas. According to its hull number, *Cestus*, made in 1964, was the twenty-first Gladiator built.

As I examined the sloop, a mystical feeling engulfed me, as if this boat had waited years for me to find and resurrect it. I recognized the boat and *Cestus* recognized me. A faint, westerly breeze sprang up, and the roar of the freeway subsided into a distant moan. I trusted with all my heart that with proper preparation this craft could take me around the wildest cape in the world and evade the islands of ice that swept past it. Because an inexorable process was already in motion, I was going to sail around Cape Horn either in this boat or one similar.

We became man and boat.

I bought the daysailer for $2,000, probably too high a price. But I was eager to move forward. This boat, with the proper preparation, could make the voyage along "the Impossible Route," as single-hander Vito Dumas called it.

Shortly after my purchase, Jack Tatum, Sr., the father of a friend, said he once sailed a Gladiator up near Anacapa Island, to the west and slightly to the north of King Harbor. "In heavy weather," he advised me, "the bulkhead can detach."

A bulkhead is to a boat what a wall is to a house. Gladiators had one directly under the mast. It was the only negative thing I heard about Gladiators.

Cestus cost me almost half of everything I had. I estimated restoring and reinforcing the boat would cost another $35,000 to $40,000. My guess was that the entire voyage would cost between $50,000 and $60,000. How would I raise that much, more than a year's earnings?

* * * * * * * * *

The days ranged from large, frothing seas with heavy wind to absolute calm.

Stalled in calms, I obsessed about eating all the food before we could reach land. Several afternoons were so still I could have lighted a candle on deck.

Then, almost without warning, choppy cold seas surrounded us. We staggered directly into the current while a bird with a four-foot wingspan soared along behind, beautifully in control, graceful against high overcast. By the thirty-first anniversary of John Kennedy's assassination, I skirted delirium while awake and conjured nightmares in my bunk. With only 39 days left, we recorded 20-mile days as the countdown clock ticked on.

Thoroughly depressed, I opened a new diary, given me at the bon voyage party by my cousin Denny's family. I wrote, "The Ultimate Run, Cape Horn -- Terror and Chaos Continued to its End: Mar Del Plata." And following that, I inscribed *Nec timeo Nec Sperno*, "I neither fear nor despise".

The day before Thanksgiving, it rained. All day we were either becalmed, cursing the fates, or overpowered with wind and struggling for control. I estimated we had sailed over 5,000 miles and for the first time I experienced a confinement attack, worse than any I had suffered at military schools or in the Marines.

The wide sea to all the horizons made the boat seem like a plastic package into which some sadistic giant had stuffed me. I hungered to stand up on dry land, maybe on a peak in the Santa Monica Mountains overlooking Los Angeles and the Pacific. Or to run down the sandy strands of Redondo, Hermosa, and Manhattan Beach with heart accelerated and eyes bugging at the local beauties. Or to drive across the high desert toward Las Vegas with dry land stretching out before me. Almost anything rather than being prisoner aboard this pitching boat and wondering about all the trouble I had gone through to experience this confinement and chaos.

By Thanksgiving, we still had approximately 2,400 sea miles to Cape Horn. Despite the discomfort from the rash, it was time to raise the spirits. For lunch, a treat -- Spam and onion. And for dinner the turkey MRE and my bottle of wine. Thank you, Cousin Denny and Jan.

Running in heavy seas, we listened to Neil Young's "Southern Man." Beyond the turkey dinner, the chardonnay, and the music, I was most thankful for the day. Because on this day, I was doing exactly what I wanted to do, I was going exactly where I wanted to go. How many of the billions of humans can claim that? And ahead lay the most exciting and greatest adventure of my life, Cape Horn.

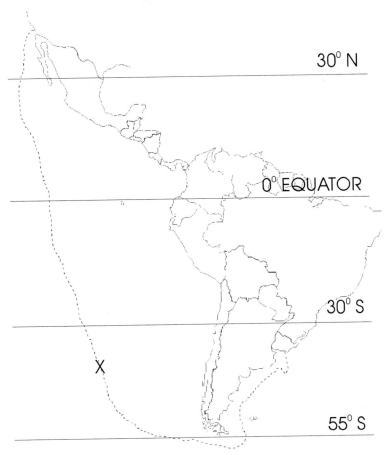

Chapter Nine

Reaching The
Roaring Forties

Tires squealing, the red-and-cream Chevy hardtop caromed around the corner onto Sepulveda Boulevard. I clutched the window frame as the centrifugal force tried to fling me into Nick, our driver. It was Hare 'n Hounds with the San Fernando T-Timers.

"We're back on track," I yelled at Nick.

"Good show, Frank," Larry shouted from the back seat over the roar of the double-exhausted V-8. "Calls for another

Country Club." Nick drove, I navigated, and Larry opened the beers. Elvis belted "Uhh, uhh... I'm all shook up..." over KDAY.

"Frank's too young," Nick called, barely making the light at the Van Owen Street intersection. At 15, I was the youngest member of this automobile club and proud to be accepted by its members, mostly guys in their early 20s. At night I was selling subscriptions to the *Valley Green Sheet*, saving up for my first car.

Larry passed an open can forward. "None for you, Nick, you're driving," he said with a laugh.

This was adventure, rocketing along on a Saturday night, propelled by Shell premium gasoline and malt liquor, windows down, enjoying the camaraderie. Hare 'n Hounds was a timed automobile event. Or that was what it was supposed to be.

Because of hot young blood and the rules of the game, Hare 'n Hounds reliably turned into an all-out race through city streets. The idea was that a lead car, the "hare," would go first to mark the course by throwing down small bags of flour several miles apart at intersections where the "hounds" were supposed to turn.

The twenty or so hounds would start about five minutes apart. Each hound was required to follow the course to the end, arriving at an average speed well within the legal speed limits. The hound closest to the predetermined average speed was the winner.

Of course, if hounds failed to see the white splotches at intersections, they would eventually backtrack, frantically searching for where they went wrong and trying to make up lost time.

"Hard left on Roscoe," I yelled, seeing the remains of a flour bag. We passed a pink-and-black Ford Crown Victoria going the other way. "Hey, wasn't that Gary?" Nick asked, a Philip Morris bobbing from his lips. "Are we lost again?"

"No," I said. "He's lost. Press on."

"Drag races tomorrow night on the Los Angeles River bed," Nick called.

"OK," I answered, searching for a flour blossom at Devonshire. We were going too fast for me to be sure, and often the marks were erased by the tires of the normal traffic.

The San Fernando T-Timers were cool guys, guys I could identify with. To many of the students at Van Nuys High, however, they were "a bad element," dropouts and ne'er-do-wells, but I felt good around them. Actually, the T-Timers had a respectable club.

Living with my father, Nancy, and my little half-brother had turned out to be awkward, and I tended to gravitate to classmates, club members, and friends.

I was turning Van Nuys High School into an academic joke.

Not all of high school was a waste. I played football on the B-Team. Our defensive line was anchored by Carl Bono and Joe Longo, flanked by Ron Tutor and Vince Tucciarone. These were solid respectable friends.

Tires screamed as Nick hung a U, and the hardtop almost capsized. "We're lost," he shouted.

* * * * * * * * * *

The night after Thanksgiving, *Cestus* ran out of control for eight hours. All I could do was huddle in my sleeping bag, listening to the murderous seas, fearing each new set of breakers would swamp us.

Reviewing my passion for rounding the Cape, I recited aloud: "Cape Stiff is the ultimate challenge. It is the Everest of the oceans. If Everest is the top of the world, then Cape Horn at the far tip of South America is the bottom. Cape Horn is my personal Everest, and rounding it will be all the reward I need."

How formal my voice sounded, something like my father's.

A sad note haunted the whirling darkness. If we survived and reached Mar del Plata, what then? What would be left? Is there life after meeting the ultimate challenge? I wondered again, would plodding about my daily routine prospecting for customers, interviewing, matching the right policies with the right people, keeping up with tons of changing regulations, conquering the paperwork, seem empty and unworthy?

By morning, the sun warmed my damp skin, but I had never felt more exposed, alone, and vulnerable. As I peered over the endless waste, some kind of message seemed in order, just in case. My hand-held radio was useless now.

I retrieved the empty chardonnay bottle from the trash bag under the cockpit. If something happened, I wanted my family and friends to know how far we got. Tearing a page from my sea diary, I wrote:

November 25
1400 hours
36° 25' south, 111° 40' west
Whoever finds this message please contact Mary Guernsey [I gave her address and phone number] Redondo Beach, California, USA to report that I made it this far. Please send this message to her, and she will appreciate it. Thank you.

Frank W. Guernsey
Aboard the sailing vessel Cestus

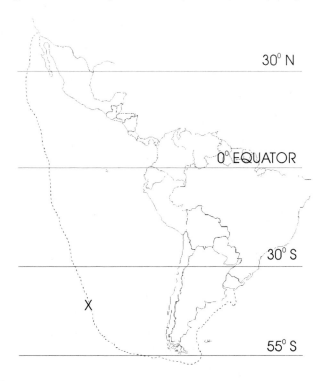

Corked securely in the clear bottle, the message joined the icy, surging Pacific.

"Bon voyage," I called after it.

Where would the bottle end? Where would I?

Gradually, the seas calmed and the next day I confided to the video camera, "I like having another day of life."

It was a routine day, relaxing, trying to dry out, pumping the bilge, making water, reading the Old Testament, playing the flute, cleaning and attempting to dry my ragged T-shirts. Peace before violence.

By 6 a.m., a full gale was lashing the waves into a frenzy, and we hove to. The wind gusted to 50 knots and the hatch slammed open, dousing my sleeping bag, making it even colder and wetter. The spray drove horizontally, and I could barely see.

Holding on below was like being inside a ping-pong ball slapped around by cranky giants. And we were only on the brink of the Roaring Forties. Every minute, the sea compelled *Cestus* to broach -- suddenly turn in one direction or another and capsize -- but she resisted.

In the morning, the intensely cold wind sucked the air from my lungs. Though saturated, my pile gear retained some of my body heat as we rode up mountains of water glinting in the dawn and down into windless valleys. At least the husky, running seas rolled in the right direction, and my guess was that we were now 25 miles north of the 40th parallel. Every eighth wave, my heart staggered as the boat lifted, teeter-tottered on the edge, poised to capsize, but never did.

I couldn't believe that as we sailed below the 40th parallel, it was like crossing a border into a new kingdom, ruled by icy water and wind that could sound like a jet in flight. On November 29, our 68th day, about 2,000 sea miles northwest of Cape Stiff, the sun scattered crystal light over a bleak world. A beautiful albatross soared effortlessly, unlike me, perfectly attuned to its environment.

The dark sea rolled off to the horizon, where a light blue sky drew a line. We were on course, free of the contrary currents, and surfing on big, running seas.

It was too much of a good thing. By afternoon, clouds appeared in the west and the wind piped to about 35 knots. As *Cestus* creaked and moaned, we raced beyond her designed speed using only the small storm jib.

Our stern would lift as one roller with enormous energy passed under us, and we'd ski along with it until the bow turned skyward and the stern down with a sinking feeling, and then the next wave would lift our stern again in a kind of rhythm that penetrated my central nervous system and kept me surfing in my sleep.

Drying a pair of socks on my stove, I noticed only two onions remained. After a lunch of dry cereal and powdered milk, I wedged into the frigid, dripping bunk and tried to read, but the violent motion made it hard to concentrate on anything but survival.

At cocktail hour, I savored a shot of brandy. The comforting warmth reassured me for the moment, but the western sky, often a work of art to end my day, looked bruised and swollen. No question, a storm was on the way. The wind didn't frighten me so much as the breaking seas. Sails can come down, reducing the effect of the wind, but there is no reducing the hammering of big seas with their spume blown away like the foam off a mug of beer.

The wind raged biting cold, and the interior of the cabin was frostbite alley. It was time for my Antarctic sleeping bag. As I nestled in, it already felt soggy and glacial. Out there in the dark, the storm jib and the steering vane kept us tracking for the Horn.

Falling into an exhausted drowse, I felt every lift of the stern, every surf downward, every rise again. Even so, I dreamed of soft, warm, lovable Mary.

When I met her in 1978, I had returned from a voyage and had just committed to another one. Dave Coffey, a bachelor friend who lived on L dock in King Harbor, insisted I come with him to meet a beautiful girl who worked nearby.

Always interested in beauty, I did, and there was Mary, with lovely, dark hair and eyes. She had an indefinable exotic look, and we fell in love. Feeling warm and tremendously close to her, I knew I had at last found my soul mate.

After a life of detachment, I bonded with Mary, and she became central to my existence. She gives meaning to my life, and when our relationship sours, as it does from time to time, my outlook changes. I begin to wither in society. Nothing seems worthwhile or productive. That's when I think about another voyage.

I heard *Cestus* call my name. "I'm foundering, Master. Help me!"

My eyes opened with an adrenaline pop. My blood pressure soared, sugar dumped into my blood, and my mind cleared instantly. We were running wild, the rig shuddering. The bow was digging into the sea at the bottom of each sleigh ride, and we were in danger of cartwheeling end over end.

Somehow, the storm sail was flapping and would soon devour itself and us along with it. The terrible vibrations penetrated my bones.

Struggling from the bag, I estimated it was about 3 a.m. The wind was whining through the halyards like a biplane in a dive. My battered knees protested as I crawled onto the foredeck. Gripping the base of the mast, I slithered forward into a cold blast.

Time and again, *Cestus* plunged her bow into the bottom of the foothills. Each time, the freezing spray stung my eyes, and I could feel my body temperature plummeting. I struggled to detach the jib halyard, then pulled with freezing fingers to lower the sail. The deadly vibration ceased.

There was nothing to do now but wait it out and pray. Back below, I shrank into the freezing bunk as *Cestus* sought her way through the seas. As we tossed, I moaned along with her. The wind howled and tried to silence my prayer, but I shouted, "Just let me make it to the Cape, Lord. That's all I ask."

We took the worst hit ever, and *Cestus* started over. I was sure her hull was crushed. Then she rose again. This was the worst night of my life, and probably the last. How the boat was holding together, I'll never know.

I recalled a prediction at my going-away party: "The man will break before the boat."

The terror continued through the night. If the crashing and howling and whining and splashing would only stop before they drove me berserk. If only the motion would ease. If only my hands and feet would warm up and I could feel the balmy breezes of Tahiti once again. But Cape Horn isn't gained by "if onlys."

We were about 120 miles north of the iceberg line. Still ahead must be worse storms, wilder seas, colder blasts, and drifting mountains guarding the Cape.

At last, dawn crept silver across the majestic seas, and the light of another day heartened me.

* * * * * * * * *

I dropped out of Van Nuys High School during the first semester of my senior year. The T-Timers became too tame, and I left them, too. Eager for freedom, I moved out of my father's house and joined two roommates above a bar named "The Runway" near the Van Nuys Airport. In those days, no jets landed in Van Nuys, but the prop planes constantly reminded us of the location.

I had achieved my ambition. Downstairs was parked a 1951 Olds, fashionably dumped. In the next four years, I would own a dozen cars, even though the authorities would often suspend my license.

The one-room apartment throbbed with rock 'n roll thundering up from the bar until 2 each morning, but it made little difference because Carl, Ray, and I seldom stayed home.

Our idea of fun was drinking till dawn by way of faked ID cards and throwing up on each other's shoes. It seemed wonderful. Drifting away from respectable high school friends, I hooked up with outcasts on the freeway to nowhere. All this booze was fueled by my job as a hung-over box boy at the Vons supermarket in Sherman Oaks.

Another pastime was playing "chicken," complete insanity. We'd drive out to deserted highways north of the San Fernando Valley in the early-morning hours. Then we'd accelerate to 60 miles an hour, steering head-on with only parking lights to mark our passage. The first driver to turn right off the road was the chicken. There was nothing more loathsome than being a chicken.

One morning when bouncing through an orange grove, I almost lost my car. I decided to look for another game. I don't even remember who chickened first.

I moved on to other roommates and other cars.

107

On one memorable trip to Tijuana, I collected six moving violation tickets. Later, with only one gear left in the transmission, I wrecked my Ford by driving into Laurel Canyon.

By Christmas of my first year of freedom, Mom returned. The pressures that had induced mother and R.L. to leave for Australia three years before had eased, and they returned to the United States, settling in New York, where R.L. became manager of Roosevelt Field on Long Island, a racetrack combined with one of the first American shopping malls.

I flew out to spend a catastrophic Christmas with them. My mother was horrified with what she saw: a wild high school drop-out, drinking and out of control.

I caroused my way through Greenwich Village on a glorious 17-year-old's debauch. Even during my hung-over mornings, it was obvious how much my mother cared for me. She tried to steer me toward a safe harbor, but I returned to California and wildness beyond measure.

The summer of 1960, I returned to New York, this time to Garden City. My debauchery was out of hand. R.L. took me aside, held me with his eyes, and said, "Frank, you're going nowhere fast."

But back in California after that summer, Tino, a friend from Delano Street, and a few of his friends drove up behind me in a borrowed Plymouth. In jest he tapped my back bumper. Playfully, I backed into him. He bumped me again and so I put the Chrysler into reverse, broke his radiator, and backed Tino, his car, and his friends several flights up the steps of city hall.

R.L. was absolutely right. Somehow, I had to stop running wild.

Freedom meant chaos. I needed some structure in my life. It was like having the emotional bends. When the external pressure suddenly disappeared, the internal pressure was exploding me.

I had made a decision.

I parked in front of a storefront downtown and pushed

open the swinging door, noting the reflection of my pale face. Behind a desk in the nearly empty room sat a young Marine in full dress blues. With a little gray hair, he could have been the commander of California Military Academy, providing a structured, however oppressive, environment.

The desk was clear except for a ballpoint pen.

He stood, a startled look on his face. "My gosh," he said, "did anyone ever tell you how much you look like James Dean?"

Dean, a legendary teen idol and actor, had died about five years before when he crashed his Porsche. "Amazing, same brooding, handsome look." The sergeant shook his head.

Glancing at his name tag, I saw "Sgt. S.J. Haub."

Smiling and shaking my hand, he introduced himself. "You've come to the right place..."

The sergeant beamed, fixing me with his blue eyes under his cropped blond hair. "We're always looking for a few good men."

"That's me," I said, hope in my voice.

"I can see you know your own mind, Frank." He pulled some papers from a desk drawer. "You're not the man to take any kind of bullshit, so I know you won't take any from me."

Right. This was man-to-man stuff. I liked Sergeant Haub.

He started filling in a form. "Your last name?" he said.

When I told him, he said, "I'm assuming four."

"Four?"

"Four years. The standard recruitment."

"Yes, I want to be a United States Marine."

Chapter Ten

Surviving
"The Worst Storm Possible"

The first of December was relatively calm, sunny and as clear as a Rose Bowl day, but bitterly cold. My image in the ship's mirror showed the raw-faced exposure of a homeless man. Constantly, I rotated my underwear, hoping for some kind of cleanliness and order. That night before sleeping, I prayed the iceberg line was dropping lower and lower, making room for my passage. Thirty days remained on my countdown calendar.

But by the time my plastic digital wrist watch recorded 3

a.m., *Cestus* was again struggling for her life. She was overpowered with just the storm jib flying, and there was nothing else to do but leave the relative damp warmth of my arctic bag and climb out on deck to douse the sail. Up in the heaving night, my hands soon grew numb, and fumbling with the line made them ache to the core. I felt fog, an icy dampness, behind the spray.

But with the sail tied down, I managed to return to my bunk and fitfully doze in the gloom, as *Cestus* roared through the Forties under bare poles. In my mind's eye, I saw the solid, floating masses, majestic and terminal, lumbering to keep their date with me.

Breath visible, I wakened to a world enshrouded in dense fog. In the churning cabin, I could almost smell the icebergs. The seas rose and continued flogging us without mercy. How had I slept through some of the tumult?

The motion was too violent for me even to make powdered milk for dry cereal. Breakfast would have to wait. The video recorder taped the seas swamping the cockpit and brave *Cestus* shrugging the water aside before swamping again. How could a craft survive this turbulence? The cruel wind berated us for the rest of the morning.

Instead of eating lunch, I struggled out on deck to set the storm sail, hoping to eke out a few miles and settle the violent movement that ricocheted me from bulkhead to bulkhead. A wave broke over us and only a firm grip on the foot of the mast kept me aboard.

Below, I imagined another five weeks of this icy bludgeoning and listened to another major creak develop in the hull. It was the wail of a lost soul, and I tried to guess what disaster it predicted. Whatever drying I had managed the day before was now soaked.

This was surely a death watch, the last day of my life.

There was utterly nothing we could do but ride it out to the end. After a few handfuls of dry cereal in the dark cabin, I reached for a tape and snapped it into my player. Fats Domino.

"I got my thrill..."

"Goodbye, Fats," I said, resigned.

The wind climbed and the seas raged, and I knew the sail had to come down once again. It was tempting just to forget it, stay inside the cabin, and accept my fate. But by sheer volition, I climbed on the deck once again. This time my hands refused to function properly. I lost the halyard, and it flew to the top of the mast.

Without the halyard, we could not fly the jib, and that would have lowered our odds of surviving.

Luckily, I had anticipated that this could happen. I probably owe my life to the spare line already mounted and ready.

I prayed in the early-morning hours for peace. But my prayers went unanswered throughout the day as the seas raged to 60 feet. The rollers pressed on the bow like a giant hand. Frothy white tops of the running seas peeped through the blowing fog.

The deck under the mast sprung a leak, further drenching my home. My throat was sore and my nose a constant waterfall. Dread would rise when a wave rumbled toward us. I'd moan along with my ship. Then the beast would strike us with its heavy paw, *Cestus* would scream, the world would turn sideways, then upright, and the agony would start again.

I dissolved a packet of MRE cocoa in my mouth for dinner and strained to maintain the will to live. My watch told me it was 6 p.m. Unless the storm relented, there was no realistic hope. I would need the courage of my old friend Mike King.

* * * * * * * * *

Just as Hillary was the hero of my youth, Mike King was a hero of my adulthood. When I first met Mike at Van Nuys High School, I recognized him as a stand-up guy who retreated from nothing. A few years later, when I was in basic training with the Marines, he earned my admiration.

113

One night during infantry training, I heard there were to be boxing matches that evening at the open-air movie arena a couple of miles from our training camp but still on base. Tired after a day of playing war games, I was nonetheless restless. Though technically AWOL, I walked the distance in search of excitement.

Probably 2,000 Marines gathered to watch the matches, rugged four- or six-round combats. Each area of the base had a champion, and these bouts were to determine the championships of the light-heavy, middle, welter, and lightweight divisions. The week before, the heavyweight championship had already been claimed and tonight the Marine champ was to fight "some civilian bozo from L.A."

He'll get slaughtered, the Marines said.

The fights were brutal. Aggression and determination made up for lack of skill. Blood sprayed the ringsiders as noses crunched and eyes puffed shut. At last the heavyweight bout. The civilian L.A. bozo, all alone, strode down the aisle and climbed into the ring. He had a towel slung over his shoulder and carried a galvanized bucket.

The Marine champion followed, an impressive 210 pounds of well-defined muscle, accompanied by his entourage and delirious cheers. His black hair bristled, and he was confident. There was something terribly familiar about the civilian LA bozo, standing alone and ready to face a mauling.

It was Mike King.

Working my way down the bleachers, I joined him in the corner, hoping none of the cadre from my outfit was present.

"Guernsey," Mike said, amazed. "What the hell are you doing here?"

"I'm an AWOL Marine. What the hell are you doing here?"

"Fighting. Will you be my corner man?"

The Marine sergeant referee called us all to the center of the ring and gave the usual "protect yourself at all times" instructions.

Back in the corner with bucket and towel, I said, "What's your fight plan, Mike?"

"Knock the jarhead out. You think I can get a hometown decision here?"

By the time the bell rang for the bloody sixth round, Mike probably held a slight edge, though it would never hold in this crowd with Marines judging the match. Less than a minute into the round, Mike dug a left hook to the body, and the Marine champion went down with a thud. As the ref counted deliberately, the fans screamed the Marine back onto his feet.

The ref inspected the tape around the champ's wrists and sent him to his corner for repairs. Precious seconds ticked away as the corner men deliberately worked at retaping the gloves. In the interim the champ recovered. With less than a minute left Mike snapped the champ's head back with a left uppercut. A thudding right cross landed on the jaw, and this time the champ didn't get up.

Mike was a gladiator, who gained the respect of every Marine present that evening.

That was the kind of courage I needed now.

Mike drove alone over 200 miles round-trip from the San Fernando Valley to wage battle as a stranger in this strange land. There was no money to gain, no glory, only self-respect and dignity. He faced unknown opponents with the odds definitely set against him. Every onlooker hungered for him to fail. No one would know of his courage, because he would never mention his exploits. That kind of courage was nobility.

* * * * * * * * *

As best as I could make out, *Cestus* was 90 miles from striking the nearest iceberg.

By 4 a.m., the storm had eased enough for me to set the storm sail again. At last the wind backed off and the seas quieted.

I spent the day in seaman's tasks. Pumping the bilge,

inundated with icy water from the storm, I found a note of cheer, a beef slice with barbecue sauce MRE, my Christmas dinner.

In wonderful contrast to the day before, sailing was actually comfortable as we hummed along on the shortened main and storm jib. The last two days had brought the most dreadful storm ever, dwarfing Hurricane Agatha, which I skirted on my way to Hawaii. In my location on the chart, roughly 44^0 south latitude and 106^0 west longitude, I printed THE WORST STORM POSSIBLE. How innocent that would soon seem.

Moving around helped me cope with the cold. My life in Southern California had hardly prepared me for the aching fingers, the numb feet, the way a frigid body ravages the brain, the watering eyes and nose, the stinging cheeks, the smarting ears, the tingling wrists and ankles and neck, the sweat inside the thermal clothes turning to ice. The cabin was colder than a refrigerator and the forepeak probably colder than a freezer.

Time to check out my Global Position System satellite navigator. I punched the buttons, but nothing appeared on the tiny screen. Though the originals had lasted two months, the new batteries were dead after only five days. I wondered if the cold had affected them.

For the next two days, we enjoyed straightforward sailing. My sea diary read, "I have evidence hope works." I was convinced that my hope for survival was so strong, we had survived "The Worst Storm Possible." I finished the Old Testament and started the New.

The realization that no one had gone before me on this particular voyage from California around the Cape to Argentina, nonstop and alone and in so small a boat, gripped me. Running the iceberg line, I played evening flute solos to Mary, Frankie, my beautiful mother and my father.

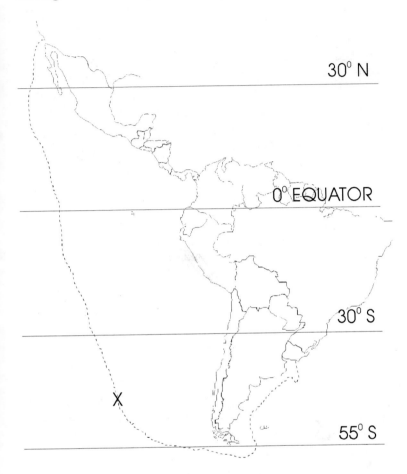

On December 7, we crossed the 46th parallel south, and I tried to gain serenity by placing myself in the hands of God.

I reckoned I could see about three nautical miles. Though keeping a wary watch, I spotted no bergs.

Then the seas began to assault us again. We were at the mercy of the seas. And time. Twenty-four days to countdown Cape Horn. I had worn the same T-shirt for 2 1/2 weeks because it was my last one. All the others had disintegrated into rags.

My sea diary for December 8 captured the condition of the seas, *Cestus* and me:

Day 77

0900. I'm tired and I'm cold and the weather at its best is bad for the boat. Having to heave to more and more to save the sails and that's when we take the worst beating. Mast is back and forth, sideways etc. Once I was thrown out of the quarter berth.... I see another 40 days of this and I really wonder if it's possible. Even the bag I sleep in is wet and you sweat in it. It's like an iron lung.... My hands are cut deeply in several areas (worry) as they don't seem to heal due to the cold and abuse. When I do a sail change and return inside they are frozen and I mean I have to thaw them over the kerosene lamp... Valleys and walls and mountains keep coming abeam endlessly and we rise and it goes under and races on and every now and then and not infrequently they break and hit and an awesome sound like a roar along with a hiss of the spray and you hear it coming and hope it doesn't hit.... The force is not describable. It's like a hammer and how this boat hull takes it is a tribute to somebody's construction....

We almost just broached. It goes right to the edge. As they used to say in the old Van Nuys High jargon we are hauling ass.

2100. The wind is out there and I'm going to try to sleep and I pray I don't get called out. I've got to let the boat run or we'll never get there and it's steady 25 plus, the wind that we don't sail in out of King Harbor and we have at least five weeks of it before us.

* * * * * * * * *

"You maggot."

The slap across my face made my ears ring. Blinking the tears back, I saw three more raw-boned Louisiana guys joining the first one.

"L.A. scum!"

I was beginning to question the wisdom of joining the Marines. Despite my military school background -- or perhaps because of it -- it was clear I wasn't cut out to be a Marine.

"Get back in line, shitbirds!" a massive sergeant screamed, and the crisis was over. Soon, cold GI clippers swooped over my head, nipped my scalp, and banished my hair. And I faced four more years of this. On the bus from Los Angeles, I found out it would have been possible to enlist for only three years.

I had signed up with the idea of saving my life by imposing some order on it, of going overseas, of attending college afterward. But as we progressed through basic training, the destruction of all individualism, I could see how naive I had been. Basic was tough after a year's diet of beer and Red Mountain wine. Except for meeting two stalwarts who became buddies, boot camp was a waste. But D.A., a red-haired guy from Glendale, and Parodi, a good-looking, blond guy from San Francisco, made great comrades. Parodi was mellow except concerning the Marine Corps. Nobody came close to hating the Marines more than Private Parodi. Luckily, we stayed together throughout most of our enlistment and remained friends in civilian life.

We were assigned to Headquarters and Service Company at Camp Pendleton. This was more like a 9 to 5 job. We were captive by day but often escaped on overnight liberties.

A pattern emerged. All day I was "Shitbird Guernsey," shitbird being Marine for misfit. I endured the happy horseshit of my job in supply, and at 5 p.m. dashed for the gate and hitchhiked to Van Nuys, some 100 miles away. Meeting the boys at the Countdown, I'd drink beer until 2 a.m., then hitchhike back to Pendleton in time for reveille.

Before long, I acquired a 1955 Pontiac and made the escape at least three weeknights and every weekend. My regular riders paid me $4 per round trip. I'd drop them off at the Greyhound station in downtown Los Angeles and pick them up at 2 a.m. for the return trip to the base.

One of the local Los Angeles institutions was the Artists'

and Models' Ball in Hollywood. Locals in outlandish drag attended this event, which was about as far from the Marine Corps as you could get.

Several friends decided to attend, and I went along, disguised as a woman under a Little-Bo-Peep blonde wig. Somehow, I ended up in the ladies' latrine, then in the Hollywood drunk tank.

The desk sergeant identified me as government property and reported me to the Marines. Soon, two disgusted MPs escorted me, still in drag, to Long Beach, and my first brig.

We were forced to live in cages with guards patrolling overhead to make sure that we stood at attention from dawn to dusk.

My behavior earned me brig time in Camp Pendleton, where at last I was permitted to get out of my costume. Eventually, I was confined to base and returned to my outfit.

Confined to base. That was beyond my endurance.

I went AWOL.

My father received an official letter from the 3rd Battalion, 1st Marines, dated 8 May 1961, and signed by Vincent A. Albers, Jr., Captain, U.S. Marine Corps, Commanding.

It informed him that "...as it is desirable that he not suffer the status of a fugitive at large or the penalties attached to deserting from the service..." he should advise me to return to Pendleton and face the consequences.

The consequences were a court martial and 30 days in the Mainside Brig. But I had avoided a bad conduct discharge.

As soon as possible, I resumed my freeway voyaging. For the next year, if I had no riders, hitchhikers would often help drive while I slept. Early one morning, I picked up a sailor in Sherman Oaks on the trip back. He was returning to his base in San Diego and volunteered to drive. I told him to wake me at San Clemente, then I fell into a deep sleep. I awoke with a throbbing brain in the back seat of my car, parked on a street in San Diego. I was already AWOL from Pendleton, some 45 miles to the north. The sailor was nowhere to be seen.

That cost me another 30 days of confinement to base.

Through it all, I had the Marine esprit de corps, but I couldn't identify with the kind of people who supervised me. By the time my enlistment was up, the Marines had promoted me to private first class four times, but three times they busted me for some failure to conform.

In 1962, our battalion moved out to Okinawa for a year and six months. Supplying myself with numerous half-pints of Jim Beam to take aboard the aircraft carrier Valley Forge, I gained a tidy sum of cash before we reached the island of World War II fame. Our base was remote in the oozing muck. There I became a seasoned veteran.

Though I still rated the "Shitbird" designation, my buddies D.A. and Parodi helped ease the pain. Every chance we got, we'd hire a cab and head for Nago, an off-limits Communist village about an hour's ride away. Nago was wonderful because no Marines wandered the streets in search of booze and women. We had that to ourselves.

The trouble with our Nago runs was that cab drivers, afraid of ghosts, refused to drive at night through the mountains and jungle. Often we were late returning to our battalion.

A muddy, rainy place, Kin, the local village, was second best to Nago. Officers were free of the hours forced on enlisted men, and often they would remain in the village to pursue our dates.

We squirmed in our barracks until one night D.A. was thinking aloud in the dark, and observed, "They're out there right now with our women. There must be something we can do."

"We ought to climb the fence," Parodi said, "and do them some serious damage."

"What?" I asked.

"We could mix up their shoes," D.A. said, inspired.

The locals insisted Marines honor one of their ancient customs. No one was permitted to wear shoes into the huts. By threatening to withhold their charms, the young ladies enforced the custom of their village, and Marines parked their shoes and boots outside. This applied to officers and gentlemen as well as to us.

In a minute we were up, dressed, over the fence and running to the village. Like demons we tore through the night, exchanging the shoes of lieutenants, captains, majors, and for all we knew, colonels. Gleeful, we broke back into captivity and slept in peace, knowing the confusion we had inflicted on the officers. To enlisted men universally, officers are the adversaries.

Eventually, the battalion rotated back to Camp Pendleton. On one of my renewed freeway voyages, the Volvo I was driving was involved in a crash. My left hand was severely mangled, and I was placed in the orthopedic ward of the Camp Pendleton Naval Hospital. For the last year of my Marine career, I lived in that ward while the surgeons struggled to reconstruct my hand.

For me, 1964 was a sobering time for thought. Some of those guys returning from temporary attached duty in Vietnam no doubt still inhabit that ward. As best I could, I joined the Red Cross ladies in trying to help out with the 80 guys in our ward, especially the paralyzed.

The next year, the Marine Corps finally awarded me that coveted honorable discharge. It's still hanging on my wall.

Resentment for authority planted at Mrs. Sullivan's and watered in military academies had blossomed in the Marines. Being a Marine did impose an order on my life and probably slowed my slide toward the abyss, but the Marines did not change my hell-bound direction. Although the military had provided the overseas experience I craved, I still was not ready for college.

My orthopedic-ward musings had shown me that when I was little, all adults were overpowering giants. Now that I was as big as anyone else, I could see the real giants were the social systems in which we live, the organizations that impinge on our lives. We'd never be free of the giants.

Knowing this would not ease my re-entry into civilian life. D.A. and Parodi would not be there to help fight the giants whose power I now resented more than ever. The civilian aftermath would make me remember the Marine Corps as a time of relative order and tranquillity, just as I would remember The Worst Possible Storm as a mere disturbance.

Racing The Ice To Cape Horn -- *By Frank Guernsey & Cy Zoerner*

Chapter Eleven

Screaming Into The Screaming Fifties

Just as entering the Forties had been like crossing a frontier, the Fifties swung open the gates to a new seascape. The waves rose higher, steeper, more powerful, and shot tremendous surges under *Cestus*. The wind rose to an eerie pitch. The Screaming Fifties were well named.

At 8 a.m. I lay awake and listened to the bitter wind as it screamed like an animal in pain. We screamed along with it, our rigging like violin strings.

Opting for speed and distance over safety, I tarried in my sopping bag rather than dousing the sail. Icebergs loomed in my imagination, forming a wall between us and our goal.

The brandy of yesterday's cocktail hour no longer warmed me. The icy cabin had seduced me into tripling my usual ration, but now I wished I hadn't yielded. I tried to visualize our position on the chart. We were about 1,400 miles from the primordial Cape, a long, agonizing way to go in the Screaming Fifties.

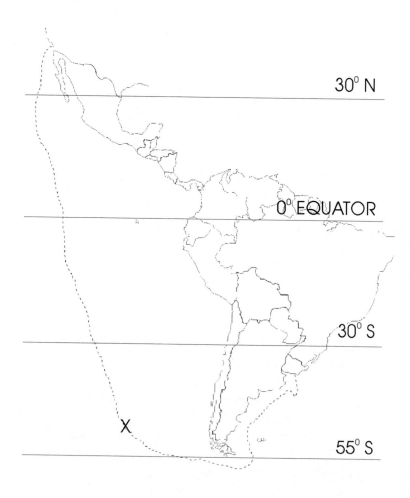

At least The Worst Storm Possible had died far behind us. Unless I completely miscalculated, *Cestus* had weathered her worst trial.

Twenty-four hours later, nothing had changed. In my frosty bunk, I was torn between letting *Cestus* track toward our goal in the wind or taking the conservative view and lowering sail. The witch's wail outside persuaded me to relent and lower the sail.

On deck, the sheets flogged me; I lost my footing and grabbed a rattling shroud to save myself. *Cestus* barreled along at hull speed under bare poles. Was this the beginning of another storm or was it par for the course in these waters?

Dark clouds scuttled before the wind, and the moon flashed across the jagged seas like a strobe light, leaving a series of freeze-action photos on my retina. In flashes, I strained to see icebergs in the emptiness.

Nowhere could I see the albatross that had trailed us for days. Did he ever sleep? I half expected to see him asleep on the wing, still doggedly behind us.

Safely below again, I pulled on my polar mittens, realizing they were ripping scabs off my battered hands. Throughout the night, I dozed and fretted about the iceberg line and my supplies. There were perhaps 20 cold cereals left. They'd be gone soon enough, and I dreaded the change in my morning routine. In a way, routine is a single-hander's best friend.

Another change would be entering the Cape Horn current. Though it would be moving in the direction we wanted to go, the seas would tower even higher. And somehow, if we actually rounded Cape Horn, we'd have to break its powerful spell to turn north into the Atlantic between Argentina and the Falkland Islands.

In the Atlantic, beyond Cape Horn, the position of the icebergs is far less predictable.

After daylight, I raised the mainsail to a triple reef, a task consuming 45 freezing minutes in the 30-knot wind.

Happily, the albatross had again taken up his station. By what spectacular navigational system had he found us? Ice sheeted all the port lights in the cabin as well as the solar panel.

I fervently wished that this was all the ice I would see. By mid-afternoon, we were dead down wind at hull speed with large following seas and a 150-mile day. In our haste, an orange cushion washed overboard. Watching it disappear in the sea frenzy, I regretted seeing something so close to me claimed by the sea.

Even so, the progress exhilarated me and I felt my will grow stronger. I estimated the nearest ice floated a safe 100 miles away. Encouraging.

The next morning, I noticed that something had damaged Leo. A large portion had been torn from the vane's rudder. That self-steering vane was life-and-death to me, and I had no materials to repair it. I could only pray for the best.

As I inspected the damage from the churning, glacial cockpit, *Cestus* lurched and I sprained my left wrist. Though it was the wrist of the hand that kept me in the Marine hospital for a year, my dexterity remained good.

Exhausted, I sat inside the cabin and watched the self-steering mechanism do its job as best it could. The albatross still tracked patiently behind us, sometimes flying low and darting out of sight behind the Prussian-blue waves, then floating aloft again and changing directions.

Was he, too, driven by a will to survive? He soared elegantly, aloof from the violence. His black-tipped wings spanned at least ten feet. Otherwise, he was white-on-white against the sky, except for a few black tail feathers.

As he zoomed closer, probably looking for a handout, I saw the pink-and-orange patches on either side of his stern head. He looked as if he meant business, and if he attacked me, he'd be a handful.

But why not share with this fellow nomad, my only companion? I found some MRE crackers and flicked them overboard. The solitary glider swooped and snapped them from the surface with his powerful, hooked beak. Then he ascended effortlessly to tack in the stout wind.

The albatross feared no icebergs. He probably used them as perches. Bergs would pose no threat to a creature with the magic of flight. For him, they'd be a mere stepping stone. He looked utterly pure and free, independent of land.

Despite the pitching of the boat, I fetched my video camera from below, determined to catch the display of grace aloft. Bracing myself in the companionway, I strove to keep the camera dry and the albatross in frame as he swung to and fro across the sky like the deliberate pendulum of an enormous clock.

I had read that these birds roam the seas for months at a time, returning to land only to breed. Not a bad philosophy of life.

As *Cestus* struggled forward, the solitary bird jerked in and out of my viewfinder. How suited he was for this harsh and lonely environment; how unlike me. Whereas the albatross could sleep on the face of the sea, I rattled around inside a hard plastic shell.

While I pumped my watermaker 1,000 strokes a day for a meager supply of drinking water, the albatross enjoyed drinking sea water, an inexhaustible supply. If every albatross that ever lived drank his fill of sea water at one time, there would be no perceptible lowering of the Pacific ocean.

Though the ocean teemed with food for the bird, I had to contend with a finite supply, hoping it would sustain me and fearing that through some slip-up in preservation or cooking it would poison me.

Mobility was also in endless supply for the albatross. Master of the air, he sailed where he willed. The bird fit into this environment perfectly, taking every advantage of it as he soared on his way, while *Cestus* and I limped along like refugees from a battle. We struggled to approximate a direction.

The bird's slick feathers warmed him in the same frigid wind that, despite my polar gear, seemed to blow through my chest and out my back.

As I blinked up at the primitive beauty, I wondered how we looked from above. Hardly beautiful. Distressed, probably, battered by the white ridges of the running seas, outlandishly out of place, scrambled in the tumult, lonely.

But most of all tiny, a speck in the infinite Pacific turbulence like an asteroid wandering in the vast expanse of the universe. From his perspective, could the bird see the plodding icebergs in the distance to starboard?

A sense of foreboding engulfed me just as Cape Horn seemed a real possibility.

By the following day, I had regained part of my confidence. I woke up thinking of Mary, and as the waves slammed, twisted, and pounded the hull, she seemed close. But I noticed an odd motion and discovered that the lines on the self-steering gear needed changing. The repair took an exhausting hour.

But the real trouble started on December 14. We had 17 days left on our countdown. At 2:30 a.m., I awakened to the violence, teetering on the edge of the berth. Clutching a locker, I avoided tumbling onto the cabin floor. My breath rattled in and out, and the frozen air chilled my lungs. Despite my cold-weather gear and the arctic sleeping bag, I was beginning to freeze from the inside out.

Before this voyage, I had no idea how the cold hurt, how it inflicted pain at every joint, how it hunched my shoulders in a vain attempt to retain a molecule of warmth, how it bit my ears, turned my feet into blocks of ice, and rendered my hands numb and useless. I wondered if the skin turning black along my index fingers was the beginning of frostbite.

My cruise down the Baja coast and voyages to Hawaii, Tahiti, and Japan had done nothing to prepare me for the cold of this Antarctic summer. In fact, the run to Tahiti was a sail to paradise. I concentrated on the memory of moderate seas, the warmth of sunshine on my face, the bath-water warmth of the spray as it flew over the bow and wiped my bare, tanned skin.

But the effort changed nothing.

I tucked my hands under my armpits but remained ready to save myself from becoming a missile. The water between my shoulder blades felt as if it were turning to ice. Outside in the tumult, ice was doubtless forming on *Cestus*.

Once I saw pictures of a sailing ship so covered with ice that the seamen were hacking at it with axes. The ponderous weight of ice could capsize a ship, and I supposed *Cestus* was no exception. I had a hammer in case I'd need to break ice. Dozing, I dreamed of *Cestus* coated in three inches of ice. The shrouds were like huge icicles.

My back ached from constantly adjusting to the pitching of the tormented boat. As *Cestus* pitched and yawed with a slightly altered movement, my back ached a little differently.

Was this farewell to the counterclockwise South Pacific current we had known since the Mentor current? Perhaps we were merging into the Cape Horn current.

Already I was concerned about breaking out of the powerful Cape Horn current into the South Atlantic, if we should get that far. Otherwise the current would circle us around the bottom of the globe like a Flying Dutchman in pursuit of my lost orange cushion.

At 5 a.m., I struggled out on deck with the wind and seas bucking, and raised the storm jib. Again the decision was between speed and safety. The wind made using the storm jib impossible, and in minutes I was back out in the chaos lowering it.

Breakfast was simple, a granola bar, because of the building seas. As I chewed slowly, tension mounted on both me and the rigging. A full gale blew, and I estimated the wind between 34 and 37 knots, whipping the seas to about 14 feet. I couldn't tell if it was leading up to a storm. Gales seemed normal in these latitudes.

Despite my bumbling fingers, the GPS calculated our position in half the time it had the day before. 50^0 02' South latitude, 96^0 20' West longitude. We had come south and east, on track for the Cape. We were roughly 1,140 miles from our goal with 17 days to cover the territory. We'd have to average 65 miles a day to be in that magic right place at the right time. To make 65 miles net, however, I was probably tacking 120 miles through the water. The Horn was within my grasp, God willing.

The wind and the sea climbed all morning. I tried to make fresh water, but most of it spilled from the bucket. Finally, I decided to save my energy. The gales had escalated to about 40 knots, with seas of about 20 feet. In my home waters, people would consider these conditions deadly. Santa Monica Bay has sustained strong gales, but they're rare and usually devastate fishing piers, penetrate breakwaters, and sweep houses in bold locations into the sea. Sailors usually have the good sense to stay in the harbors during such winter gales.

Every five minutes, enormous waves lifted us on their backs, washed over us, and changed our course by moving Leo's paddle, still functional despite the missing chunk. The seas increased to about 24 feet, and the wind was in a full gale.

In a weird attempt to control it all, I decided to reduce everything to videotape. I pointed the camera to stern and captured the turmoil of the seas, a sight so unreal it could have been from a distant planet.

I taped the GPS calculating our location. It took 10 full minutes conversing with the satellites before it confirmed our position. Were we so far south that the GPS required extra time to find our coordinates? Probably not. But what if it were malfunctioning, what if we were dangerously close to the icebergs, perhaps just over the three-mile horizon?

While I was taping, another cushion, a sponge, and the lid to the kerosene lamp were swept overboard. The floating cushion was extra baggage anyway. How long could a human survive in these seas, with or without a lifejacket? Thirty seconds, maybe.

Despite the storm, the albatross followed us throughout the day, and his company comforted me. I had come to believe that nothing bad could happen to us as long as we were under his watchful eye.

Feeling uncivilized by swigging from the brandy bottle, I observed cocktail hour below decks. Desperately, I wanted to survive. Most of all, I wanted to see Mary and my son again. I wanted to run on the beach while the surf crashed and the gulls fussed. I wanted the camaraderie of the Redondo Beach Yacht Club and the Tuesday night beer can races.

According to my new custom, I shared crackers with the albatross. The seas grew larger and threatened to bury us. Tons of water were poised to suffocate us.

Looking through the portlight was like peering into an aquarium, straight toward the bottom. The wind shrilled at more than 40 knots and the rigging rattled horribly. The seas escalated to over 25 feet.

Hoping for some sleep, I climbed into my bunk. The seas slammed against the hull, and I trembled and vibrated with every agony of the boat. A wave broke over us and I was back on the floor. A storm was coming. It was so brutally cold, my kerosene lamp made little difference. There was nothing to do but wedge myself into my bunk and try for some sleep. I had given up on preparing dinner.

By 8:30 p.m., I realized the gale was becoming a storm. During the storm we barely survived 12 days ago, I had reached the limit of my competence and *Cestus* had reached the limit of her endurance. If this storm surpassed that one, we would surely perish.

* * * * * * * * * *

My hand froze on the Chrysler's door handle. I heard heavy panting in the pitch black. Something was wrong. As I eased the door open, an unearthly snarl exploded and something grazed my ear. I struggled to close the door before the lunging beast within was upon us.

"Run, Shelly," I shouted, but she was already gone.

I dashed into the West Covina alley and ran for my life.

133

Screeching, Shelly ran ahead of me toward Roger's car waiting at the other end of the alley.

My return to civilian life in December of 1964 had been rough. When the pressure of the military suddenly disappeared, I was running out of control again.

I needed help, but my father was building a house in Malibu, and my mother was living in New York. Going to them would have seemed like surrender anyway, because most of all I wanted independence.

Jobs eluded me, and I had no place to stay. Floundering, I had called a high school friend, Roger Bacon. The son of an accomplished writer and prominent columnist, Roger wanted to become an actor.

Unlike some of my other friends, he was gentle and peace-loving, and he was kind. Roger was courting Rachel Mendoza, whose friend, Peggy Pacheco, was willing to lend me her living room couch. Peggy's beau had just recently been released from jail. He did not share Peggy's amiable heart and was severely annoyed. But before the conflict got out of hand, he robbed a bank and soon was caught, after generously distributing cash to friends and strangers alike.

My friend Phil, with whom I had stayed when I was AWOL from the Marines, had a kind mother who came to the rescue before more problems could develop at Peggy's. Mona owned several homes and she provided a small, two-bedroom place in Sherman Oaks for me to live.

I moved in with another friend from Van Nuys High days, Vince Tucciarone. Our budgets were so tight that we labeled our eggs to keep our food separated. To add to our problems, Phil liked to return with various girlfriends and use our rooms for his rendezvous. Though we padlocked our rooms when we left, Phil, undeterred, simply ripped the hasps off the wall.

I finally landed the job repossessing leased automobiles. In a way, the job was fun because it required ingenuity. Finding a car among the millions in Los Angeles County is no mean feat. And once it's found, it must be reclaimed. The night we tried to repossess the Chrysler, we pried the locked garage door open far enough for the elfin Shelly to slither underneath and open it for me.

Besides being fun, it was a risky business, because most of the lessees had little enthusiasm for returning the delinquent cars. Placing vicious guard dogs inside the cars was just one trick. Another time, a disgruntled "client" -- forewarned by his brother -- confronted us in his garage and waved a large revolver in my face. Not all repossessions were successful. But the pay was good.

The career of a repossessor seldom lasts long, however, because it leads nowhere, and imparts only a good working knowledge of how to steal cars. It was time to get serious. I got a job parking cars at the Beverly Hills Hotel.

Sadly, R.L., my stepfather and mentor, died about this time, and my mother moved back to Los Angeles. His death saddened me because he had truly cared about me.

Not wanting to park cars forever, I enrolled at Los Angeles Valley College under the GI Bill, hoping an education would lead to a substantial life. Working the main entrance of the Beverly Hills Hotel, Tucciarone scored all the good tips while I labored in the bowels of the parking structure.

Though the pickings were meager, I could now afford a car, and the basement of the parking structure provided a great place to study.

At the Barrel, a favorite watering hole, I still engaged in exemplary dissipation after work. One night, a friend and I headed to Casitas Canyon about 100 miles away for some informal road racing in my Triumph. Tearing along the sinuous road with a Porsche trying to pass us, I lost control, bounced along a guard rail, destroying my beautiful TR4, and came to rest just short of plummeting off a cliff.

Hours later in an emergency room, it dawned on us that the Triumph was full of beer cans. That would look suspicious to any investigators. Still wrapped in our bandages, we made our way to the junk yard where the wreck had been towed.

Because it was Sunday, the yard was closed, and we'd have to climb the chain-link fence. I barely managed to outwit a pair of nasty-looking Dobermans and escape with the beer cans. But I could see it for the nonsense it was. I was a college student and a 24-year-old veteran. I had to sober up and mend my ways. It was time to settle down.

I landed a respectable job at the movie studios, and began hanging around Malibu with Phil and Ortega, who would take me for my first sail several years later aboard his small catamaran.

My most distinguished film was "Who's Afraid of Virginia Woolf?" My contribution was to turn light switches on and off at the proper time. It was also important that I remain remote and quiet. The first requirement, I managed. But during one of the few quiet scenes between Martha, played by Elizabeth Taylor, and her college professor husband, portrayed by Richard Burton, I leaned intently over the scaffolding and my pen fell from my breast pocket right onto the set. I never heard a louder clatter.

"Cut!" shouted director Mike Nichols.

Everyone looked up at me. Dismay. Frustration. But no one chastised me. Patiently, they reshot the scene as my ears burned.

During my studio career, my mother married a man with the unusual first name of Mage. In some respects, he resembled R.L. Mage also took interest in my progress and, like R.L., he was a powerful businessman. Mage was a solid man who had a solid influence on my life.

Earning my associate of arts degree pleased Mage so much that he offered me a trip to Europe and a new Opel Cadet to drive while there. The proposal couldn't have come at a better time, for my wanderlust was calling me away from the exhausting Southern California life, and my anthropology courses had whetted my curiosity about foreign cultures.

Those four months in Europe were my first experience

in foreign places entirely on my own. I had traveled fast enough that none of the baggage of life caught up with me. I would never forget that compelling sense of freedom.

Home again with serious intent, I met a lovely young woman named Sharon, who moved in with me in December of 1969. The next July, I earned my bachelor's degree in anthropology from San Fernando Valley State College, now California State University, Northridge.

Mage may have been enthusiastic about my education, but he was horrified that Sharon and I shared quarters but not marriage. Though large portions of American society were accepting living together, Mage believed it degraded both Sharon and me. In my heart of hearts, I agreed with him, and I certainly did not want to lose his respect.

Sharon and I married. In keeping with my new maturity and armed with a college degree, I searched for employment. This time, there would be no box boy jobs, no repossessing cars, no parking lots, no switching lights on and off at the studios. I was a respectable married man, living in Redlands, California, and soon to be a father.

I made a good impression during my interview with the Ross Labs Corporation, producers of the baby formula Similac. The interviewer was a man in his early 50s, impeccable in a dark suit and tie. I felt the compression of a tie around my own neck.

The man looked up from my application, pushed his bifocals up his nose and said, "Guernsey?"

"Yes, sir," I said.

"Like the cow?" He smiled.

"Yes, sir."

"I like that. It projects a wholesome image. It associates our product with a natural process. It should make you the perfect salesman for Similac."

He was a prophet. I was Salesman of the Year for 1971. Two years later, I made the transition to insurance. At last I had found my niche.

But while I gained a profession and a sense of direction, I lost something precious. After three years of marriage, Sharon and I parted without bitterness.

Sharon returned to her native Rockford, Illinois, with little Frank. One month later, she returned to live because Frankie missed his father. I turned to Roger Bacon, who was living in Hermosa Beach, near King Harbor, and Little Frankie and I moved into his bachelor pad.

Soon Roger's little nephew Dougald needed a home and he moved in with us. It was something like the Odd Quadruplets.

I mourned the death of our marriage for a year, then I put it behind me.

I bought a sailboat named *Boogie* and moved aboard it on L dock in King Harbor Marina.

Ten years had passed since I left the Marine Corps.

Chapter Twelve

Outliving The
Ultimate Storm

December 15, Countdown to reach Cape Horn: 16 days.

Just after midnight, I jammed myself between the bunks on the cabin floor, my elbows braced against the side-to-side thrashing, but nothing stopped my insides from rising into my chest as we hurled airborne over the top of a wave.

Sleep visited only in groggy fits. The wind screeched like a bandsaw, then was muffled as *Cestus* slumped into the huge valley between waves. The hull creaked and groaned, and the rigging howled and tried to break loose.

Then it was as if a volcano erupted directly under our keel. It didn't seem possible, but this was worse than The Worst Storm Possible in power, authority, intensity, in any way a storm can be measured. I was certain there was no way we could survive. What would I call this storm?

Prematurely, I'd already used "the worst storm possible." Maybe I'd call this the "ultimate storm," because it was beyond the worst possible.

In the tumult, something banged my head. My hair felt stiff and wiry as I rubbed it. My back ached and my saltwater wounds throbbed as my body chafed against the floor.

At 6 a.m., I ventured out into the cold and discovered that the albatross was gone. Surprisingly, I was not. Loneliness tied knots in my throat.

The seas were unbelievable barbarians. Streaked with foam, they ran thick and mountainous with long, breaking swells.

I checked the GPS and was horrified. We were at 51^0 21' South latitude and 94^0 58' West longitude. We were making almost due south, too much south. Too much toward the icebergs.

When I tried to adjust, *Cestus* ignored me. Current and wind were sweeping us toward the silent ice mountains.

Hebrews 12:1 came into my head. "Let us also lay aside every weight ... and let us run with perseverance the race that is set before us."

I must simply go with the flow, I knew. Even so, we had sailed 80 miles in a day, though sailed is too weak a word. Driven out of control before the sea and wind is more accurate.

About 8:30, as if by a supernatural command, the wind piped down. The seas remained large and thick, about 26-28 feet, a little higher than *Cestus* is long.

Thank God. The worst of it was behind.

The wind had moderated to 25 knots.

We were about 52^0 south, and I jibed the triple-reefed main. I was sure we had reached the Cape Horn current. An immense following sea rose behind us, possibly forecasting another escalating storm. I knew that only if the wind remained moderate would the seas subside, but the wind continued to climb, pushing to 35 knots.

As I taped sea conditions, I commented to my high-tech companion, the video tape recorder, "December 15, my eighty-fourth day out of Babylon." It was a slip of the tongue. I meant Avalon, but from the purity of the Southern Ocean, Southern California did seem like a center of wickedness from which we've sailed over 6,000 miles, with about 1,080 remaining to

Cape Stiff.

There was no relief. The wind piped to about 45 knots.

The raging seas made civilized dining impossible. I had dry beef jerky and raisins for lunch. Meals would not be possible until the seas calmed. Worse, my sore throat made swallowing difficult.

I tried to pump the watermaker, but the motion of the boat made even that simple task dangerous. I could easily have slipped and banged my already-battered hands.

The wind continued to gain, and the sea was almost completely white, with long, thick cables of foam blanketing the surface. In all my years at sea, I had not seen anything like it.

By 6 p.m., the storm was blowing at 50 knots, and the waves seethed and fumed at *Cestus*.

To celebrate Christmas Eve, I found the bottle of Jack Daniel's among my medical supplies and sipped it until a sense of well-being warmed me. I left most of the bottle for the future.

The waves were climbing to awesome heights, twice as high as the mast. I figured quickly, 60 feet, higher than a six-story building, a magnificent yet horrifying sight in the Antarctic twilight.

I struggled from the cabin floor into my bunk. My body, trying to retain warmth, tensed in the sleeping bag. My head ached for the first time during this venture. How could I have a dry cough in this water world?

Suddenly, the world disintegrated. *Cestus* staggered and lurched drunkenly. My fears of doom rose once again.

And once again, *Cestus* persevered. The steering vane had flopped loose, but otherwise, we were intact.

For the first time on the voyage, anger tore at me. Over and over again as I struggled to repair the vane, the seas doused me. I raged against my impotence. Cold to the bone, my hands would hardly obey me. My eyes stung from salt, and I squinted to work with the stubborn parts.

The wind continued to bully the seas into higher peaks. The rush down into the valleys turned my stomach giddy. My last cushion washed overboard.

Anger made the repair job more difficult.

I had to remind myself, God wasn't shaping the Southern Ocean just to frustrate Frank Guernsey. The cabin floor was awash, but I struggled back into my bunk and hung on.

Suddenly, a stupendous wave broke over us like a fist driving us to the bottom. Water pushed in, and I felt we were submerging into a watery tomb. Two violent movements and we surfaced. I heard the banshee shriek of the wind. By its sound, it must have been reaching 60 knots and, judging by the eternal roller coaster, the seas must have topped 70 feet. But we were still afloat. The mast and the rigging had held. Bruised and battered, *Cestus* scudded before the wind like a leaf. I breathed once more, and coughed yet again.

I rubbed my temple and felt a small knot, but no blood. In that moment of feeling that it was all useless and the voyage was over already, the never-ending pain, sound, violence, uncertainty, and absurdity pushed me close to the edge. I shouted incoherently, then speech returned.

I barely heard my voice recite parts of Psalm 23 in the savagery:

"The Lord is my shepherd: I shall not want. He maketh me to lie down in green pastures: he leadeth me beside the still waters... Yea, though I walk through the valley of the shadow of death, I will fear no evil: for thou art with me; thy rod and thy staff they comfort me...."

"Dwelling in the house of the Lord" might come sooner than I had wished, but I was resigned to God's will.

* * * * * * * * * *

December 16, Countdown to reach Cape Horn: 15 days.

I awoke just after midnight to an eerie sound like the air raid sirens I'd heard in World War II movies of the bombing of London. Or maybe it was during a prison break in an old gangster movie on late-night TV. A mournful wail slowly rising to a scream. Or maybe it was the sound of all the fire engines I ever heard as a little boy.

Nature was sounding the alarm.

As the siren wailed to a crescendo atop a wave, the seas hurled me onto the floor. *Cestus*, plaything of the violence, rolled far to port. The port windows were under water.

What could I do but pray?

"God, please save us. Please let us survive, if it is your will."

I could hardly hear my voice as tons of sea water thundered over us, threatening to uproot the mast.

There would be no sleep again tonight.

Sometimes mini-hallucinations visited, then another wave thundered over the hull.

I still could not make fresh water, and there probably would be no meals, either, as long as the storm raged. If my estimate was correct, I had lost 15 to 20 pounds.

I began going over the necessities. I would need to get some sail up and keep tracking toward the goal at all costs.

The storm would not let me rest. It dumped me, like a sack of potatoes, onto the floor again. For awhile, still in my arctic bag, I wedged myself in a fetal position between quarter berths. Then I battled my way back into my bed. And the seas loomed higher.

The day ahead looked just as bleak. With the siren wailing, there would be no listening to tapes. No flute playing in the frozen, tossing cabin, and no dolphins to play for. No albatross to watch. He had deserted us. No cocktail hour. No videotaping. No bailing. No photo taking. Nothing but hanging on and praying for deliverance.

An hour later, I plunged from the bunk again, then lay on the floor, bruised and hugging my knees to my chest. Icy water swilled around me, but I was too tired to care.

I took out the GPS at 8 a.m. to check our location. The tempest had blown us about 40 miles in 24 hours in a southeasterly direction, putting us farther from Cape Horn than the day before. At least the storm had blasted us away from the iceberg line.

If we failed to make Cape Horn in the next 12 to 14 days, there would be no hope. I didn't need a GPS to tell me that.

I peered from the portlight straight into the deep. As *Cestus* righted, I could see an almost completely white sea, mountains snowy with foam. I had never seen anything like it, and I hope I never see it again. The seas were malevolent, and I was sure the winds were gusting at hurricane force.

I braced myself and stuck my head up into the doghouse for a better look. The breath stuck in my throat. Not only did the seas flow white, but through the spray the frenzied mountains appeared almost four times as high as *Cestus* was long. The monsters must be 80 feet, I thought. I tried to picture an eight-story building.

The seas were almighty, wondrous, killers. If the death of this salesman struck in the next 10 seconds, all would be worth this terrifying sight.

My face banged the aft port. Rubbing my nose, I retracted my head from the doghouse and took up my post on the floor again.

I must accept that death can come any second, I told myself.

Any second... any second. *Cestus* swooped down an immense wave and, at the bottom, stuck her nose in. The stern rose and we were ready to cartwheel. But instead of going end-over-end, she sloshed to port and instantly we rose on a giant elevator as the siren wailed louder.

We held on for another half-hour before we faced the prospect of cartwheeling again. My eyes twitched and I couldn't control them. I must accept going northeast until the world changed, if ever, and we could track toward the Cape again. I knew, to round Cape Stiff, we needed to drop to 57^0 south. We were past 52^0. We need to make east longitude, too.

Would the torment never end? Twelve hours later, I was still braced on the floor. The cramping was unbearable. My muscles ached from holding myself in place between the bunks. As the water swirled around me, I knew I needed to bail, but the boat's movement was too furious.

When the cover on the aft storage compartment blew open, I prayed it would not be carried away. Sea water would swamp the boat. I would have to abandon my hiding place and secure the hatch before the storm claimed it. The hatch was only a few feet from the doorway, but I would have to work against the strong forces in the boat and get back before we took another hit and the cabin filled with water. Visibility was close to zero as I emerged from the cabin.

With haunting visions of the orange cushions going overboard, I tied a loop around my waist and secured it to the step. Then I edged out on knees and mitten-clad hands to confront the storm. Ice foam crusted the cockpit. I caught the edge of the hatch awkwardly and slammed it shut. I could barely hear the closing over the noise of the sea. The next sound was my body smashing against the deck as a wave slammed into me. I felt as if a crane were hoisting me into the air. I felt myself being carried out into the fury like the cushions before me. My life depended on a fragile wooden step.

My breath whooshed out as I slammed into the cockpit floor. I scuttled crab-like back into the cabin and took up my sentry position on the floor again. Water on the cabin floor formed a tiny, violent ocean of its own. I thanked God for the miracle of life even for a few more minutes.

I had given up on asking God to spare me. After three days of living in this watery hell, I had accepted the inevitable. I was almost serene. So much so that I actually dozed for a few seconds at a time and my body joined *Cestus* with the flow of the enormous waves.

We were now on terror watch. The only point left in this life was to see how far we could go, to survive another day, for no other reason than to see what happened next.

Perhaps it was only my fatigue, but near midnight, the siren call of the wind at the top of the waves was diminishing. Was the storm dying? Or was I?

* * * * * * * * *

December 17, Countdown to reach Cape Horn: 14 days.

At the top of the mountains, the whine of the wind and the strumming on the rigging was easing, giving the illusion that the storm was subsiding. I was almost lulled into believing that the worst was over, when a hulking wave washed over us. Twenty-four hours ago, it would have been minor among its brothers. I estimated it was 40 feet.

The violence was definitely easing, but it was still almost impossible to get up off the floor and back into the bunk.

After two hours of feeling and hearing the retreating storm, I realized that I might be able to make sail by morning.

At the peaks of the waves, the sound of the wind indicated 50 knots or less. Everything's relative. When the winds first rose to 50 knots and the seas to about 40 feet, I thought we'd perish in minutes. Now they seemed almost like old friends returning from a journey.

We probably were out of the storm and back into a strong gale category on the wind scale. In an hour, the wind dropped another 10 knots. *Cestus* punched on through the night.

I thanked God that, even though off course, we so far had avoided the path of the icebergs.

I curled up on the floor and managed to drift off to sleep. By daylight, I felt much better. Searching the cabin, I found a can, possibly the loose cannon that had hit me on the head. Searching farther, I located granola for breakfast. The taste of grain on my tongue and the weight of food in my stomach convinced me I was in everyday life rather than life after death.

Layers of anxiety peeled away as optimism returned. It was time for another list. I ticked off my concerns:

Time and position. Despite the effect of the storm, we

were still in striking distance of our goal.

Icebergs. A constant concern. At least so far, none had bashed us.

Weather and sea. There's no question that the back of the storm was broken and we would be able to hoist sail before long.

The boat. Miraculously, it had lived through a beating that was once beyond my wildest imagination. Most of the water aboard had not come through the hull but from the constant deluge topside. Hard to believe that the mast and rigging stood firm. *Cestus* was showing me that she could take any punishment to complete the voyage. I knew, however, that the storm could have fatally weakened the hull.

Food. If anything, the storm had been a benefit. Simply too battered to eat, I had saved meals for the future. As the seas subsided, however, hunger returned.

Water. The easy motion of the boat now allowed me to use both hands to make water.

Equipment. A survey was in order. But with the mast still standing, I was encouraged that all else was working also.

Heath and mental health. Still holding on. My forearms and thighs looked scrawny, and there was no doubt I'd lost weight. And there was no question that if I had had to endure another day of the storm, I would be over the brink to madness, unable to distinguish reality from hallucination.

I had found the limit of my endurance.

I crawled back into my bunk and enjoyed the sheer luxury of stretching out. I awoke two hours later to seas no more than 30 feet. I glanced out the hatch to see dark-blue seas topped with white foam streaks. Blessed relief.

The wind was probably still at a gale, but I decided to make sail. I put up the main sail at triple reef, along with the storm jib.

We were on course for Cape Horn once again.

As I looked back toward the subsiding seas and gray clouds, I saw life. First just dots in the sky, two enormous albatrosses flitting back and forth.

"Hello, friends," I shouted. "Welcome back." My huge grin cracked my lips.

Was the bigger one my old friend? Surely it was. And the other one, a mate? What a good omen they were. I found some MRE crackers and tossed them to the waiting birds. My elated shouting revealed the depth of my isolation: "Hello, there. Welcome back."

I scanned the horizon to starboard and saw no sign of icebergs.

I checked my electronic navigator. As I suspected, we were far off course, but still only about 930 miles from Cape Horn and making good speed in that direction.

Hunger overtook me at noon, and I indulged in Ramen noodles. Then I had to be about my tasks. I bailed gallons of sea water from the bilge; my reward was to see that no new water replaced it. We were definitely still in business.

I sensed how paranoid and jumpy I was becoming. Early in the afternoon, a squall struck, and for a terrifying moment, I was sure the storm had returned. But the wind piped to only about 40 knots, then subsided. I sighed in relief.

By late afternoon, the weather had begun its assault again. Huge, following seas almost overtook us several times. I dropped the main sail and relied on the storm jib. Squalls continued to pound us. Ice foam constantly blew off the rim of the rollers. Through it all, *Cestus* was making about four knots toward the Cape.

The trembling and anxiety seemed to surface from nowhere. I was exhausted, and my knees buckled when I tried to stand. Like a case of the shingles, fatigue pierced to my nerve ends. My rash resumed its torment. Hunger and thirst suddenly gripped me, as cold again punctured my chest.

In my exhaustion, I felt oddly cleansed, serene. I had escaped the world of locks and keys for a more fundamental life. Before I left, I needed mental and emotional restoration, and the storm had given me that. Gone was the emotional roller coaster of life ashore. I had found purity and, God willing, I'd return a better human being.

I had escaped the consumer society -- house, pool, car, mortgage, and things, things, things. All I'd ever want again would be a good boat. The raw experience of this storm had blessed me with the sight of nature at its most beautiful in the remotest seas of the planet.

If death comes now, I thought, it will be after the greatest adventure of my lifetime. If not, then rounding Cape Horn will be. I prayed, "Dear God, please bend your laws so we can do the impossible within the next two weeks. "

Chapter Thirteen

Running The Iceberg Line

A new owner, I sat in the cockpit of the *Boogie*. We were comfortably tied up in slip 16 on L dock of King Harbor Marina. The *Boogie* was a fiberglass sloop, an old Columbia 26 Mark I, previously owned by my friend Bill Hiney, who worked as an art director at one of the studios. Often I crewed and cruised the Channel Islands with him. I had bought the 26-footer for day sailing in Santa Monica Bay.

A haze of fog lent magic to the scene as I listened to the

slight ping of unrestrained lines against the masts, the music of the marina. I was 33 and my marriage was in shambles. Little did I suspect that the next three years would be some of the happiest in my life.

L dock was populated on the north by large and mostly expensive power and sail boats. Just across from my more modest slip was the *Aphrodite*, an elegant CT41 ketch, 41 feet of grace and beauty. Her clipper bow faced ours.

Along my side of the dock were mostly sailboats under 27 feet. Still behind me was the part of L dock devoted to smaller boats, daysailers, mostly.

The *Boogie* was the first home I ever owned. Here young Frankie, now 3 years old, would stay with me every other weekend and one night during the week. It was good to be aboard.

The gate to the gangway banged, and a thin man with brown hair strolled down, pausing to place a package on deck of the *Aphrodite*.

He stepped over to my boat, smiled, and extended his hand. "Welcome to L dock," he said, "My name is Dick Darling. You see my boat over there. We're neighbors. Will you be living aboard?"

I introduced myself and assured him I would be his neighbor.

He possessed a kind of sovereignty of nature, a certain bearing of a gentleman. I would always think of him as "Richard."

He accepted a glass of wine and he filled me in on some of my neighbors, an interesting lot, ranging from medical doctors to entrepreneurs.

"You picked a good spot, Frank," he said. "You'll find a number of divorced gentlemen on this dock, including me. We all play hard but, make no mistake, we all work hard, too. Even though our watchwords are camaraderie and debauchery, you'd have to say that L dock really has a work ethic."

He said he was a Purdue graduate, a metallurgist for

McDonald Douglas. "You'll find, Frank, that on L dock, ladies are appreciated more than, perhaps, anywhere else in the world." He smiled. That sounded good to me.

There was no doubt I would be in good company. When Richard went back to his boat, I glowed with a sense of well-being.

The residents of L dock lived deep in the culture of boats, sailing and planning cruises. They talked boats and loved to share adventure tales. Their idea of a holiday was to sail to Santa Catalina, Anacapa, and the other Channel Islands.

I divided my life, working away at my insurance business and living the life I loved at L dock. I liked the people and adapted easily to their lifestyle of responsible hedonism and adventure. These were the congenial people, who, in their sometimes eccentric ways, formed a cohesive colony. Before long, my dockmates referred to me as "Captain De Bauche."

Their acceptance pleased me. I was living in a family, and I basked in their acceptance and warmth.

Of course, a captain must sail, and the weekends without little Frank found me day sailing in the bay, honing my skills. Richard Darling, brandy in hand, often instructed me in the sailor's lore and offered sage advice on the human condition.

Before long, I was venturing to the far reaches of Santa Monica Bay. The first overnight trip – and my first experience with weather -- was to Paradise Cove, about 23 miles to the northwest shore of the bay. My crew was my insurance associate, Barrie Gile, and my date, a French girl, who unfortunately spoke no English.

We had hardly cleared the mouth of King Harbor when a gale blew us back in. Barrie went home, but the next morning Natalie and I reached Paradise Cove to anchor for a perfect evening.

My second cruise to the Cove proved more challenging but less successful. This time, crew consisted of Barrie, my cousin Di, and his friend, Michael Dunn. We intended to sail to the Channel Islands Marina, around Point Dume, in Oxnard,

California, spending the first night in Paradise Cove.

We reached the Cove without a hitch, crowded into a tiny inflatable for a dinner ashore, and returned to the *Boogie* wet and happy for an early-morning departure. Setting an anchor watch, I went below to sleep.

Di's scream awakened me. I dashed onto the fog-shrouded deck, and managed to see a Malibu local dashing down the beach with our little inflatable. The anchor watch must have dozed while the local swam out and shanghaied our dingy.

Our life raft gone, I held a vote. There were two votes to return to King Harbor, but as Captain De Bauche, I asserted my authority. We would push onward to the Channel Islands Marina in Oxnard, roughly 24 more miles. Luckily, despite the fog, we reached our goal and sailed back to King Harbor the next day.

I liked sailing with a definite goal from point A to point B. It was far more satisfying than day sailing, which involves leaving the slip, sailing around for a few hours, and then returning without ever really going anywhere.

The longer I lived on L dock, the better acquainted I became with the citizens living there. There were young, healthy, intelligent, and fun-loving people on that dock, and I developed affection for each one. All bore distinct characters. Tarzan Tom lived across the dock aboard a 22-foot boat, and he often paraded around in no more than a G-string.

Dave conducted a vicarious affair with the lady at the end of the dock whose husband was pursuing Joline, who lived nearby aboard a Westsail 32. The affair never emerged from Dave's dreams, but he was smitten.

Mike lived aboard *Dirty Harry,* a beautiful 45-foot Chris Craft power cruiser. Although he was cordial, he stuck to a group of friends.

My friend and nemesis Bruce lived on Punk Dock, as Captain Darling had dubbed the dock behind us. One morning without permission, he snuck aboard the *Aphrodite* and was making a long-distance phone call when Captain Darling returned. The captain exploded and drove Bruce back to Punk Dock. The two men never spoke again.

Less than five years later, Bruce would ram me in the slip and damage my steering mechanism before I departed on my single-handed cruise to Hawaii.

Bob Cringan, who later would be of tremendous help in preparing *Cestus* for the Southern Ocean, was planning a sailing trip with his lady, Carmen, aboard his Lapworth 24 to Costa Rica.

John, a doctor who lived aboard a 45-foot Alden yawl, loved to gamble. He practiced medicine in Wilmington, an area of Los Angeles, and many of his patients were on state assistance. As a diagnostic procedure, John would hook patients up to his Nano-Ray machine, resplendent with banks of flashing lights.

Supposedly, John could interpret from the way the lights flashed the ailment of his patient. The story was that even if the bogus Nano-Ray machine actually worked, so many bulbs were burned out that it was useless anyway.

Much to the preoccupation of my dockmates, Martin, a dock neighbor, located a beauty who sunbathed with her girlfriend on the deck of his boat. Both were topless. Not that we were peepers, but Dave and I would position ourselves to peer through the portholes of several boats to make sure the young ladies were all right.

There were married couples who lived on L dock, and there were residents who kept to themselves and did not join in the everyday revelry. Everyone was part of the community, however, and everyone joined our convivial dock parties.

A Denny's restaurant down the San Diego Freeway was a convenient spot for me to meet clients from Orange County. After one such meeting, I came out to the parking lot and noticed Mike and an associate between two cars.

When I walked over to say hello, I saw more money in their large suitcase than I had ever seen in one place in my life.

Mike didn't seem at all embarrassed. Unexpectedly, the next day, Mike gave me two terrific tickets for the Lakers basketball game.

In a coincidence years later when I sailed to Tahiti, I met Mike in the art museum that displayed the only Gauguin on the island at that time. He was with a girlfriend and amiably invited me and Mary, who had flown to meet me, to dinner. I never did ask him about the suitcase.

These were the congenial people, who, in their sometimes eccentric ways, formed a cohesive colony on L dock. Only now can I see my love for them is rooted in the sense of family they gave me. I basked in their acceptance and warmth.

The satisfying months rolled by and my sailing skills grew as I logged more sea miles: Santa Catalina Island, about 24 miles from King Harbor, and the Channel Islands about 65 miles from my home port. Santa Cruz, Santa Rosa, and even Anacapa Island seemed far off shore at the time.

* * * * * * * * * *

December 18, Countdown to reach Cape Horn: 13 days.

Now that the storm was dead, every dawn I kept an iceberg watch. This was the 87th day of the voyage and I was thankful that *Cestus* and I both lived. Scanning the horizons with my binoculars, I saw nothing but the endless Southern Ocean.

Though I lived hour by hour, my immediate goal was to survive till Christmas.

The question still was, "Will God let us pass?" Our chances seemed better since the seas had mellowed to about 10 feet and spray no longer blew from the caps of the waves. The water was an icy blue.

The GPS fixed our position at 53^0 South latitude and 91^0 West longitude. A look at the pilot charts assured that we were about 70 miles from the red line of the icebergs, advancing on them but still a safe distance unless there were such a thing as rogue bergs that failed to follow their predicted paths.

The wind fell to about 35 knots, relatively mild compared with what we had already experienced. All we could carry was the storm jib, probably from now on.

I went through the chaotic cabin and restored everything to pre-storm order. While I was bailing, I found a loose MRE, with cherries and candy. It was amazing how such a small thing could cause excitement.

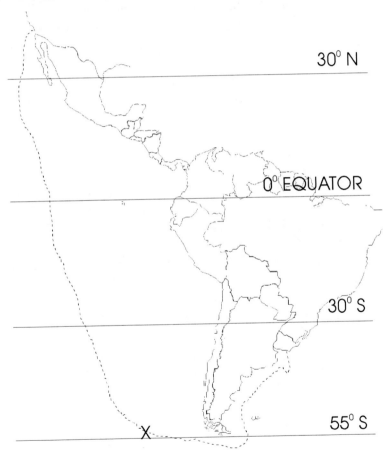

As I turned the MRE pack over in my hands, I saw how torn, bruised, and scabbed they were. They were the hands of an old man in a desperate struggle. Nothing I did spared them, and my mittens, though necessary in these temperatures, tortured them.

Constantly squinting toward the horizon hurt my eyes, but I couldn't stop obsessing about the icebergs. Sometimes when I first glanced up, I thought I saw one, but the binoculars revealed it was a phantom.

During the afternoon, the seas came up. If this was the beginning of another storm, it would be our last.

Just as I was about to grab my flute and dedicate "Yesterday" to my father, a wave jabbed us abeam, knocking us down. "Please, God", I prayed, "don't let it be a harbinger of a storm. We've had enough."

* * * * * * * * *

December 19, Countdown to reach Cape Horn: 12 days.

When I inspected the bilge, I discovered the water level had risen. I fretted, was it possible that we had cracks in the hull? Bailing worked my hands into open wounds again. I checked the hull, but could find no cracks. The water had to be coming from someplace.

The GPS placed us over 800 miles from Cape Horn with 12 days to get there. According to my calculations, the ice was about 50 miles to the south. The wind fell to about 15 knots and we sailed well with the triple-reefed main and the storm jib. I wished it would last.

But the sea is tricky, and by 11 a.m., we were completely becalmed. Stopped. Not a whisper could I detect. Not a bird in sight. I hoped it was not the calm before another storm.

Even if the calm forecast no storm, we were dead in the water when we should have been tracking to the Cape. All I could do was monitor the horizons for icebergs and pray the wind would return.

I dined on my last onion, still strong enough to make my eyes water. Garlic was now the last fresh food aboard. Since the storm, my strength had built slowly. But I was frail compared to the man who had sailed from Redondo Beach an eternity ago. Being at sea 88 days made me think a lot about eternity.

My heart leaped when a new, large pair of sea birds approached. More companions! They seemed smaller than the wandering albatrosses, but they also took up their posts behind us and waited for crackers.

Late that night, I lay in my bunk, my teeth chattering. I'd been so wet and cold for so long that I feared pneumonia. I couldn't remember the last time I was dry and warm, but I knew it was long before the storm, even before the first storm.

As I lay there, I listened to the sails slatting as *Cestus* rocked in the calm sea. I knew a delay like this could be fatal. Once again, I had the ethereal feeling that we had actually been consumed by the storm and that these last few days were an unrelenting life after death.

* * * * * * * * * *

December 20, Countdown to reach Cape Horn: 11 days.

In the early-morning calm, a haze of ghostly ice mist rose lazily from the surface. Immobility nailed us down. If it was the calm before a storm, it would be a massive storm.

In spite of deep weariness, I tried to remain alert and keep a constant ice watch. We were in the crucial stages of our run to the Horn, and the ice could steal our victory while it was almost in sight. All I asked was to see the Cape, if only for a few seconds.

The fix for the day suggested a nightmarish thought: We might sight bergs soon because we were now actually south of the iceberg line. Each hour we drew nearer our goal, now just over 780 miles away.

I spent part of the morning going through the boat, tidying my gear, and discarding what I didn't need. Biodegradable debris went overboard. The boat was now down to bare bones. I noticed as I worked that the unnerving calm had one benefit: My hands were getting a rest from my frantic labor. They badly needed healing.

Cocktail hour brandy braced me. Maybe I should stop dreading another storm, I chided myself. Maybe I did have one more storm left in me. Though I probably don't deserve it, I thought, maybe the Good Lord will just sail me in without too much pain.

Or maybe I'd had too much brandy.

Breathing the cold fog seared my lungs as I listened to Streisand and Sinatra tapes. I was saddened to find that some of my tapes had snapped, probably from the cold.

* * * * * * * * * *

December 21, Countdown to reach Cape Horn: 10 days.

There was daylight about 20 hours a day now. As a slight breeze ruffled the sails about 5 a.m., I went out into the frosty air to check the steering gear and rearrange the main sail. *Cestus* responded and doggedly moved east.

Gallons of water in the bilge disturbed me and bailing continued to take its toll on my hands. My theory that *Cestus* took water through the seam between the hull and the topsides didn't hold in these relatively moderate seas because she didn't spend much time heeled over. The fiberglass has been so worked, water could be seeping in anywhere. Maybe it was gurgling up through the seam at the keel.

My morning check of the GPS showed we were within 720 miles of the Horn with 10 days to get there. We would have to average slightly over 70 miles per day. Unless some wind returned, we'd never make it. Time was running out. The window of opportunity would slam shut with us on the wrong side of it.

Cestus had been beaten almost to death, and each day I felt my stamina drain. If for no other reason, I wanted to reach land to nurse my ravaged hands.

* * * * * * * * * *

December 22, Countdown to reach Cape Horn: 9 days.

It was the beginning of the Antarctic summer. Freezing, I went on deck and tacked the boat to east-northeast. We reached slowly with little strain on the rig.

The long days worked to our advantage in keeping the iceberg watch. If there were bergs present, they were beneath the three-mile horizon.

Around breakfast time, I felt movement. Thank God. The wind rose to about 15 knots and we were underway again, tacking truly toward the Horn.

We had barely begun to move when I thought I saw an iceberg hard to starboard. Something was shimmering on the horizon, but visibility was poor, and even with my binoculars, I wasn't sure what I was seeing.

Many smaller birds now suggested we were close to land. Chile lay 400 miles or so to the east.

By 8 a.m., the wind was blowing in squalls. My morning fix put Cape Horn about 660 miles from us. This clean wind, smelling of the vast Southern Ocean, still offered us a chance.

Three hours later, I could see that the current had definitely turned north. I adjusted the steering and sail trim, and *Cestus* felt the strain. We couldn't afford to be swept up the west coast of Chile. Allowing ourselves to be pushed north by the powerful current would doom our mission.

* * * * * * * * * *

December 23, Countdown to reach Cape Horn: 8 days.

A wave flicked me from my bunk, and I bashed my head on the corner of the sink. I felt blood oozing hot onto my chilled skin. I had the odd sensation that my brain might finally be breaking loose. Using the heel of my right hand as a compress against my temple, I felt the blood trickling down my forehead.

But I didn't have time to coddle my injury. Still bleeding, I triple-reefed the main.

The bleeding was relentless. After four hours, I slapped tape across my head to keep my brains in and hoped it would hold. Moving my jaw made my temple throb, and the red of blood everywhere concerned me.

I checked our position. Once again, we had dropped below the iceberg line, an uncomfortable situation, and we now had ice to the north.

Despite the squalls, no storms had struck again. The storm track was headed north in December, just as the ice was headed south. If one of those storms that sweep across the Southern Ocean toward Cape Horn this time of year should catch us, the voyage would be history. Along with the icebergs, the storm track was a key factor in calculating the window of opportunity.

Large waves began to pound us around noon. If the third storm developed in Drake's Passage as I rounded the Horn, there would be no survival.

During my afternoon filming, I explained to my camera that I needed stitches in my head, but Band-Aids would have to do. I hoped I would survive to see the tape. I was curious about how my head looked. Praying that my skull wasn't fractured, I decided not to take further risks by sleeping in the bunk. From now on, I would curl on the floor near the anchor and hope we didn't flip over. If we did, the anchor would impale me.

During the evening, I toasted a pair of socks on the cooker and put them on. The dry warmth embraced my feet.

Late into the night, as I lay awake, I fretted about my head wound. Was my skull cracked? I had no double or blurry vision, and that was probably a good sign. I decided to leave my head alone until we finished the voyage. Knowing the wound should be cleaned, I feared only breaking it open. For the moment the blood had stopped.

Racing The Ice To Cape Horn -- *By Frank Guernsey & Cy Zoerner*

* * * * * * * * * *

December 24, Countdown to reach Cape Horn: 7 days.

We were 532 miles from Cape Horn with a week to sail Drake's Passage clear of ice and before another storm could sink us. We must average just over 75 miles per day, a feasible distance if all else -- the wind, the hull, the rigging, the current, the storms, the watermaker, myself -- would hold.

This was my hope on this Christmas Eve. We were pushing toward the culmination of five years of planning and preparation and 15 years of single-handing. It was thrilling.

As noon approached, the swells grew higher and thicker. Any weather at all and they would be as immense as they were during the height of the storm. We didn't want to face 80-foot walls of water again. In addition, we had once again dropped south of the ice line, and bergs could be mixed into a storm brew.

The swells loomed almost dead astern, tempting me to sail farther to the south and then round up so we would be taking them always on the quarter. That course would place us in the ice flow, however. I considered the choice for three hours, then decided to stick with our original course, avoiding the ice, a greater danger than the following seas. We needed to finish the voyage because the boat was beaten and I was hurt. My stamina was ebbing; I felt weak.

It was 7 p.m. when the wind rose to a gale. Before I could douse the main, we almost lost the rig. *Cestus* crashed on under the storm sail.

As I counted the 13 cold cereals remaining, I ate the last chocolate bar. I lay on the floor and thought of Christmas and rising hope.

I sensed Cape Horn drawing closer while *Cestus* drove forward like an inexorable force. With each moan of the boat, with each hiss of the wind and sea, we drew closer. I became conscious of the pumping of my heart. Wild exhilaration, wilder than the seas guarding Cape Stiff, elevated me to a new level of being.

* * * * * * * * *

December 25, Countdown to reach Cape Horn: 6 days.

Late in December, King Harbor stages its annual Christmas Parade of Boats. Anyone with a powerboat or sailboat is invited to enter.

To entice sailors into the considerable effort and expense of decorating a boat, there are prizes for the most beautiful decorations.

The boats parade up and down the harbor, turning back before the eyes of hundreds on the massive tourist pier. It's fun to drink brandy in the 50 degree Southern California winter and hear the kids cheering as we putt by.

After the parades, we convene at the clubhouse for drinks served by Santa and tales of high adventure around the Christmas tree.

How I missed that camaraderie this Christmas night, 7,000 miles away. The Redondo Beach Yacht Club seemed light years away.

I thanked God for our progress till Christmas. My new goal was now Cape Horn, the root of the world.

Chapter Fourteen

Winning The Race

December 26, Countdown to reach Cape Horn: 5 days.

When I awakened at 3 a.m., squalls were sweeping over us. I checked our course, and *Cestus* was sailing due north. There was no choice but to go out into the Antarctic blast and heave the boat to. Traveling north away from our goal was deadly with so little time left.

Circling the horizon at dawn with my binoculars, I spied ice specters that dissolved on second inspection. So far, my luck held.

My GPS indicated we were about 400 miles from the Cape at 8 a.m. The average remained about 65 miles per day, if everything else stayed the same.

Unbelievably, the temperature continued to drop. The cold forced tears to stream down my cheeks as I stamped my feet to encourage circulation. Although I was constantly tempted to rub my wounded hands together for warmth, I knew the disaster that would follow.

Several more albatrosses took up the vigil and I rewarded them with crackers. For amusement, I broke out the video recorder and tried to follow their swoops. I noticed that the gray cloud layer lent a somber look to the seas.

By noon, we were popping along. Looking over the charts was downright exciting. With continuing luck, we would soon sail off the chart we'd been using for over two months. I couldn't remember when we had put this much sail up. After several false alarms, we must be in the Cape Horn current at last, according to my charts. There was hope.

As I pumped the watermaker, I saw an odd disturbance on the surface of the water. I scooped a bucketful and, to my amazement, saw a swarm of tiny, shrimp-like creatures. The longest were about two and one-half inches.

Krill, whale food. Whales with baleen instead of teeth sift krill from the water, and I marveled at the astronomical number it would take to keep a whale going for even one day. Rather than deprive a whale of dinner, I emptied the bucket overboard.

A little later, I saw about 25 yards off to port a calm patch of water that looked like a whale's footprint.

Just before sunset, I took an electronic fix and saw we would soon pass 56^0 South latitude.

* * * * * * * * * *

December 27, Countdown to reach Cape Horn: 4 days.
The early-morning iceberg watch revealed only the usual

disturbing illusions. Bergs appeared in the corner of my eye, but when I looked directly at them, they disappeared. The longer awake, the more likely I was to see these ghosts.

The GPS fixed us deep within the Cape Horn latitude. We had four days to make about 330 miles. The Horn was still within our grasp, if a storm in Drake's Passage didn't end it all.

All was going well except the current. My charts clearly showed we should be in the Cape Horn current, which would boost us toward our goal. Instead, we were bucking a current, sailing well against it, and probably netting about 2 knots, only 48 miles per 24 hours, hardly more than half of what we needed to round the Cape in the open window of ice and storms.

Strangely, after all the days of storms and rough weather, the day was mild and hauntingly beautiful. The afternoon clouds painted the placid sea an unusual shade of silver. My GPS confirmed that we sailed at 56^0 South latitude.

The air felt warmer in the faltering wind, but as the wind dropped, *Cestus* slowed.

We tried to eke out a few miles with the main and working jib both at the second reef point, but by dinnertime, *Cestus* rested dead in the water. Or so it appeared. The current was perhaps pushing us back. Under 300 miles from the prize, everything stopped, and I wondered what would come next.

My mind skittered off on bizarre, abstract planes, and I had to concentrate to bring it back. I wondered if the unreality were connected with the throbbing of my temple, which I had been trying to ignore all day. I thought I saw a whale rolling his back above the surface, but I wasn't sure, and for the first time I talked to myself without the excuse of the camcorder. Not bad, I supposed, after 96 days alone at sea.

Sunset at 11 p.m. encouraged surreal thoughts, and I tried to combine the dark and the rocking boat for brief hours of sleep. But to my delight, the wind came back up, though it kept me awake after setting a reefed main and jib.

* * * * * * * * * *

December 28, Countdown to reach Cape Horn: 3 days.

I was up at 4 a.m. again, but there were no icebergs this dawn. The rising wind forced me to skate the icy deck and reduce sail. But then it puffed itself out.

When the wind rose again three hours later, I was on deck to set the reefed main and jib. Would the weather hold, I wondered. Too much was at stake for it not to.

The sea responded to a 15-knot wind, and *Cestus* romped toward her goal. My morning fix put us about 60 miles from the Pactolus Bank, to be avoided because the bottom rose from over 4,100 fathoms abruptly to 22 fathoms at the bank, and vicious seas resulted. Yet the wind and current were setting us straight toward this hazard. There were still about 280 miles to Cape Horn.

Just before noon, we managed to avoid the bank by sailing to the north of it. What an irony it would have been to avoid the ice, only to wreck on the Pactolus Bank so close to fulfilling my life's ambition.

The gray overcast dropped lower, with patches of china-blue sky peeping through. In contrast, the sea was almost gun-metal blue.

By mid-afternoon, the wind was up to about 18 knots and we were sailing well under reefed main and jib. An hour later, big, running swells were behind us. I tacked to sail through Drake's Passage, the body of water between the Horn and the Antarctic continent. This put the wind on our starboard beam. *Cestus* sailed well with such a wind and, besides, running dead down wind through these swells could well prove treacherous.

And at last we sailed in the flow of water that would hurry us through Drake's Passage to the Horn -- the Cape Horn current -- after so many false starts. I learned that when mariners enter the Cape Horn current, they will know it because of its swiftness and power. There's no mistaking it.

If only the weather will hold, I thought, we should make it in two days.

Out of brandy, I took a sip of the Christmas/medicinal Jack Daniel's to toast the weather gods.

* * * * * * * * * *

December 29, Countdown to reach Cape Horn: 2 days.

On this 98th day from California, I kept an all-night watch for icebergs, fighting sleep and dozing for only fitful minutes at a time. Dawn revealed a dull, gray sea. The air was so cold that an iceberg could have been near. Perhaps it would have been even colder without the low, gray overcast.

I expected to see land for the first time since California -- Diego Ramirez Island. It lies south and west of Cape Horn, but it is apart from Terra del Fuego, the 27,000-square-mile archipelago Ferdinand Magellan named the "Land of Fire."

Small birds were swarming everywhere across the surface of the relatively mild waves, a great improvement from the storm.

My 8 a.m. check showed we were about 30 miles north of the Pactolus bank and actually below the line of icebergs. Our position precarious, we had two days, three at the most, to make it before the window of probability slammed shut on us.

There was no doubt we had entered Drake's Passage. According to the GPS, we were making 7 knots, a goodly speed for my tiny craft. It wouldn't take long to go far.

Big, rolling swells pushed from behind just before noon, but no storm was in sight. Our luck was holding.

A large flock of albatrosses arrived for their late-morning feeding. They now restricted their visits to morning and evening.

An hour later, I calculated that in three hours we had rolled along 21 miles with the current. *Cestus* was eating them up. We were bent over with a stiff, freezing wind, and *Cestus* continued to fly. The overcast lifted so that I could see the horizons, and patches of blue sky peeked through.

Later in the day, squalls passed over us. Rain beat on the cabin top, and once again we were being pounded. The good thing about squalls is that they hit and pass you by. Storms last forever.

After a few late-afternoon sips of Jack Daniel's, I lay in the bunk, hoping I wouldn't go flying again in the night. It's impossible to wear a football helmet for sleeping, but there had been nights I had needed one. I grabbed a much-needed nap, then was up again for an all-night watch.

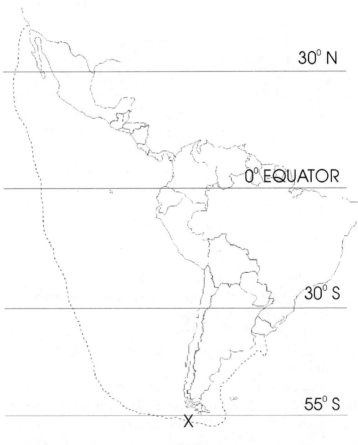

* * * * * * * * *

December 30, Countdown to reach Cape Horn: 1 day.

Off and on during the night, I listened to a Frank Sinatra tape, but I dozed for longer periods than I intended. After dawn, when I scanned the horizon to the south for ice, I saw nothing, not even the usual apparitions.

My 8 a.m. GPS check showed we were on the scary ice line of approximately 57^0 South. Before long, it would be necessary to decide if I should tack north to get closer to the Cape for better viewing.

Too far and I could get grounded on the Cape, an ironic end to my voyage. The beauty was my timing. If all went well, tomorrow we would sight the Cape, and from that moment, we'd be on our way home.

By 1 p.m., we were about 60 miles from Isla Diego Ramirez, just west of the Horn. That might be our first landfall, our first sighting of land. Even the rising weather and need for Mylanta did not dampen my enthusiasm.

Using my GPS, I determined we were making 7 knots. The GPS measures our speed over the bottom and not through the water, so the swift current accounted for much of our progress.

For the next four hours, we maintained 7 knots. This close to land, I was betting my life on the electronic GPS. Approximate fixes out at sea are fine, but this close to land, the anti-environment of my boat, positions must be determined precisely to avert disaster, especially now with about only 5 miles of visibility.

It was squally, but in my eagerness, I let *Cestus* run under sail.

The cold had accumulated in my body from long exposure. The kerosene lamp was my one glimmer of heat, but it was giving me coal-miner's black lung, I knew. Nonetheless, it was most welcome as it neared midnight.

* * * * * * * * * *

December 31, Saturday, Countdown to Cape Horn: Victory!

"A light!" I shouted.

Keeping watch all night from the doghouse had paid off. To the north shone a beacon right where Isla Diego Ramirez should be. I glanced at my watch: It was 2:30 a.m.

My heart pumped. First it was years to the Horn -- years of preparation and struggle -- then months, then weeks, then days, and now it was down to hours. If God permits, I assured myself, we should pass Cape Horn today, precisely in the middle of the window of possibility. My guess was that we'd feast our eyes from about 20 miles out.

Sailing well, *Cestus* splashed north through the eastbound current. In this part of the world, the current equaled our top speed so that if we tried to sail back to California, the best we could do would be to hover over the bottom. At worst, we would be sailing west while actually moving backward.

A nerve-wracking thought: The current was so swift and heavy that it would be easy for *Cestus* to broach. Another: What if the weather socked in and we swept past the Cape without being able to see it? Would God let that happen after five years of struggle?

The beacon on Diego Ramirez had blended into the dawn. I strained, but could not see the island. But today I should be able to raise the Chilean outpost atop the Cape with my VHF radio. How good it will be to hear human voices.

Not wanting to miss anything, I sat in the frigid cockpit for breakfast. Thank God, the overcast rose at the horizons. Under the jib and the reefed main *Cestus* pushed the seas aside confidently. If my calculations were correct, the next landfall would be Ila Hermite, one of a group of islands just to the west of the Horn.

A few hours later, at 10 a.m. precisely, landfall rewarded

my patience.

I went below, found the video camera, and climbed on deck. Leaning my back against the mast so that I could use both hands on the camera, I started taping. The zoom lens captured Hermite dead ahead. Even though the boat was relatively stable, it was almost impossible to keep Hermite framed.

Desperately I hoped to be capturing this moment to share at the Adventurers' Club and with the sailors of the Redondo Beach Yacht Club. Though I could see Hermite Island clearly with the naked eye, it might be obscure on the tape.

The more I stared through the telescopic lens, the more excited I became. The smudge on the horizon was like a signpost pointing to Cape Horn.

In the midst of my concentration, a small rogue wave smacked the port side of the hull, I slipped, and started to tumble overboard. My left hand shot out with the camera, and my right groped for the starboard shroud. Slashing my hand on the wire, I saved myself -- without even a foot dipping in the water -- and regained my position.

That was terribly close. Unable to know I was overboard, Leo would have steered *Cestus* onward until she went aground on the southern tip of South America, probably never to be found. With the temperature of this water, my agony wouldn't have been long, but I took deep, thankful breaths as I hugged the mast.

Looking at the deep red line added to my scourged hand, I felt nothing, and again trained the camera on Hermite Island, but it now had disappeared into a mist. Carefully, I climbed into the cockpit and went below for my GPS and charts.

I located Hermite, actually made up of four islands, one named Isla Deceit. That island easily could have deceived me if I hadn't for years burned the profile of Cape Horn into my dreams and waking thoughts.

A disconcerting paragraph jumped off the page of my pilot book: "9.04 Ice in the form of bergs and floes is to be found throughout the year in the S part of the South Atlantic

Ocean. It is impossible to give any distinct idea of where ice may be expected. It frequently happens that one or more years may elapse during which the route around Cabo de Hornos will apparently be free from ice...."

God, make this one of those years.

"No rule can be laid down to insure safe navigation, as the position of the ice and the quantity met with, differs so greatly in different seasons. Vigilance is urged when crossing the iceberg region."

The South Atlantic still lay ahead.

The pilot book offered a black-and-white profile of Cape Horn, the same one etched on my brain.

Taking my VHF radio, I climbed back up on deck to lean on the mast and gloried in the fact that *Cestus* was sailing like a dream. Despite the way the voyage had worked the sails, they were drawing like crisp wings with the wind from our starboard beam. To the left of the jib, a vague gray image loomed.

Cape Horn!

My perception soared, and my entire body reacted as if to morphine. The pain diminished and an exultant pleasure grew until I could hardly contain myself. What an awesome, gut-wrenching feeling. For years, I had anticipated this moment. What a glorious landfall.

All landfalls are sweet, but this one was ecstasy. For this I had sailed from California 100 days ago. For this I had raced the icebergs. For this I had risked my life.

Relief and joy and pride in *Cestus* and a terrible poignancy overwhelmed me and I shouted, "Thank you, God."

And for one of the few times since leaving Mrs. Sullivan's School, I wept.

Finding my tape of a flute solo of "Amazing Grace," I let my emotions flow into the music, which represented my deepest feelings.

Before the voyage, I had copied words by Fraser Heston in the front of my sea diary. As I reread them, I at last truly understood him.

"There is something magnificent about Cape Horn. It is a place of elemental power, of primordial energy; wind, sea, rock, ice, rain, sun. All in perpetual motion and conflict, and also in perfect balance. To navigate a small craft around the Cape ... is one of the most challenging and exciting experiences a yachtsman can ask for. Cape Horn. Cabo de Hornos. Cape Stiff. The name resonates with legend."

For another half-hour, my back to the mast, I could do nothing but stare at the 1,394-foot cliffs. I was still about 25 miles at sea. Breaking the spell, I keyed my VHF radio to Channel 16, the hailing and emergency channel.

"This is the sailing vessel *Cestus* calling Cape Horn. This is the sailing vessel *Cestus* calling Cabo de Hornos..."

Only static.

"This is the sailing vessel *Cestus* calling Cape Horn. Can you read me?"

A voice responded in Spanish. I did make out "Cabo de Hornos," so I knew my transmission was successful. My own Spanish is tentative, not any more accomplished than most people who grow up in Southern California. I did know numbers, though, and I made out that he was repeating latitude 55° 59' South and longitude 67° 12' West.

When he slowly and distinctly asked my name and nationality, I could tell he was cordial and making a good effort to communicate with me.

In my limited Spanish I said, "My name is Frank Guernsey. I am American, Cabo de Hornos. Over."

From this point on he called me "Francis."

As best I could make out, he asked my port of departure, and I responded, "Redondo Beach, California." He repeated "California" several times and so did I.

After a pause, he asked if it were in the United States. He thanked me and inquired about my port of destination. He did not repeat Mar del Plata, Argentina. Talking to this friendly voice, even in Spanish, was a thrill.

175

He asked my speed, I thought, and I answered that it was approximately 7 knots. Then he asked the size of my vessel and when I responded with eight meters, there was another silence.

He repeated this request and I repeated my response. A silence followed, and I thought we had lost contact. But he came back on, repeating eight meters. I confirmed.

Our communication became more difficult, as if he weren't sure of what I was saying. He asked how many aboard and another silence followed when I told him. He said he was alone, too.

If my Spanish served me, he said he couldn't see me through his binoculars. He asked me if I could see his antenna on the east side of the island and I couldn't.

"God keep you, Francis."

Since we were barely communicating, I knew that asking him to contact Mary would be futile. Although disappointment welled up, talking to another human left me numb for awhile. What a weird experience it seemed. Although he was alone, he was essentially different from me. He was acting as part of an organization, part of a bureaucracy, probably the Chilean navy. I was free of all that. But getting back to civilization -- God willing -- might be more difficult than I anticipated.

As we drew closer to the Cape, I fetched the video camera again, and said things like "Land's end, literally; boys, I'm tired," and "This is the best I could do."

Staring at the Horn through the lens, I felt something that Heston failed directly to mention about Cape Horn. It is a holy place. In quiet conversations over the years, friends have told me about the aura of such places as Stonehenge, Civil War battlefields, and the rim of the Grand Canyon. I've encountered the rare holy places myself a number of times, always on the ocean. There had been days there so warm, beautiful, and serene that they surpassed all temporal experience.

One friend claimed that as he stood on the narrow beach at the base of the monolith forming Point Conception, the "Cape Horn of California," he felt the spirits of the thousands of

Chumash Indians who had used it for a burial ground.

My feeling was similar, the awareness of spirits.

Perhaps the spirit of brave Dutch Captain Willem Schouten and his brother Jan, who made the European discovery of the Cape in 1615 aboard the *Eendracht*. They had sailed from the city of Hoorn in Holland. On sighting the Cape, Willem yelled, "Cape Hoorn." The sailors took up the cry, no doubt thinking of their homes. With a little modification, the name stuck.

Or maybe it was the spirit of the thousands of men who sailed windjammers around the Cape from New York to San Francisco in the days of the California gold rush. Many a brave man and vessel foundered off the Cape in the struggle into the Pacific.

Or maybe it was the spirits of the yachtsmen that made Cape Horn a holy place. The first yacht to sail around the Cape was *Pandora*, a 37-foot ketch manned by two men. It sailed from Australia in May of 1910. Connor O'Brien and crew followed aboard *Saoirse* in his world-circling cruise from 1923 to 1925. The first single-handed yachtsman to round the Horn was Alfon M. Hansen, a Norwegian, who sailed a double-ended 36-foot lifeboat, rigged as a sloop, from the Atlantic to the Pacific, bucking the horrific current all the way.

Like those who went before, I faced the same challenge: getting home. At the bottom of South America, we were roughly 1,300 miles farther south than the Cape of Good Hope. The South Atlantic stood between us and Mar del Plata, some 1,000 miles away. After sailing around Cape Horn in my own boat, even the thought of going home was a letdown, but it must be done.

Racing The Ice To Cape Horn -- *By Frank Guernsey & Cy Zoerner*

Chapter Fifteen

Dodging The
Deadly Overfalls

"Humans!"

The handle of my precious watermaker stopped in my hands. My eyes strained at the black speck on the gray, watery horizon. The misery from the open saltwater sores I sat on winked out. As I switched on my video recorder, my only companion since I set sail, I repeated, "Humans? After all these months alone..."

I glanced at my watch. It was January 2, 10 a.m.

In my excitement, the watermaker clanked onto the fiberglass cockpit floor, just missing my foot. I reached inside the cabin for binoculars. The glasses revealed hardly more than a dot, but across the placid long swells, the dot had the vague shape of a boat.

"Yes!" I shouted into the desolation.

It was easy to anticipate the life aboard the oncoming ship -- a capable captain, a jolly crew, heated cabins, the smells of hot food wafting from the galley, spotting my small boat, coming to investigate to see if they could give me assistance. They'd have warm, dry bunks to sleep in, hot food, so much fresh water they could drink all they wanted, and probably even shower in it, dry clothes. Their boat would cut through the water, unlike my craft, thrashing in every wave, sapping my energy just keeping my balance. I couldn't wait to see their smiling faces and waving hands, hear their surprised voices shouting at me, an unlikely sight in these waters.

Though I wouldn't board, I'd certainly have a drink with these fellow mariners. Camaraderie here in this most enormous wilderness on earth would be sweet, human contact and all that human contact means. How I would love to hear human laughter again.

"No!"

Not after being so close in this great ocean.

Was it my eyes? Was the speck turning away?

Frantically, I keyed my tiny VHF marine radio.

"This is the sailing vessel *Cestus* out of Redondo Beach, California, calling the motor ship. Can you hear me?"

Only white noise. I knew my radio was working. I had talked with a lone Chilean close ashore only two days before.

I desperately needed this vessel, because my tiny radio transmitted only line-of-sight, relatively few miles across this wilderness. I was aching to let my wife, Mary, and my family know I was still alive. Any boat except mine this far off the traditional course would carry powerful single-sideband transmitters that could relay my messages back to the world.

About 80 miles east of Cape Horn, the silent gunboat left my entreaties unanswered. It circled closer and closer in the long, glassy swells, a hostile menace. I hadn't endured over 100 days at sea through calms and storms, surviving most treacherous seas, to fall victim of a pirate.

Clack-clack. I injected a slug into my shotgun.

The gunboat stopped about 200 yards away. If there were to be a confrontation, it would be now. The thought of a fight was ludicrous. Fighting is against my nature.

Besides, the mysterious boat probably had me outgunned 10 to one. It could probably blow us out of the water with hardly a trace.

The birds cackled. The huge albatross floating nearby ruffled his feathers.

Face to face, *Cestus* and the gunboat rode the gentle swell.

Then, as its engines muttered, the gunboat belched greasy smoke from its stack and started in a straight line back toward the north .

"Call my wife, Mary," I shouted into my VHF. "Call my wife."

I tried to swallow my disappointment, a lump in my throat. There were still countless miles to sail to Mar del Plata. But we were around the Horn! I reflected on Dumas's comment, "It was lunacy to attempt Cape Horn alone, in a 9-tonner -- barely that." What would Dumas say about *Cestus*, barely 3 tons. Instead of speculating, however, I'd inventory my remaining resources for survival. As I did so, a cold fog swirled around us.

My rashes were healing, but my weight loss was a concern. My left temple was healing without stitches, and I didn't think it was infected. Still, it could tear open again if I smashed my head in another ejection from my bunk. Along with my strength and endurance, my supplies had diminished as the days of the voyage lengthened. However, it was now a warm day and I was drying out and recuperating.

Though my mind had been close to the edge during the four-day storm, it continued rational thought. It realized that the letdown after the tremendous excitement of reaching Cape Horn was natural and that I would soon focus on the new goal of reaching Argentina.

Despite my disappointment with the gunboat, we might sight boats between the Falklands and Argentina with skippers willing to relay messages to Mary. So far, I wasn't the victim of unbearable loneliness; and even though I had come close to the limit, I felt my emotions would remain intact till we reached our destination.

Cestus was leaking but still afloat. She had stood up to an incredible beating, especially during the two storms. During times of mental stress, I had speculated that the cold water might make the fiberglass brittle, but that worry proved groundless.

Cestus still tracked a true course through the water, guided by a steering vane with a chunk out of its oar. The rampaging seas had applied incalculable stress on its stainless, aluminum, fiberglass, wooden, and plastic components. And even though the wind had warped the vane and required my attention, the Scanmar Monitor showed no signs of quitting.

Miraculously, the rigging had resisted snapping, and the spars -- the aluminum mast and boom -- appeared undamaged. It was possible, however, that *Cestus* felt as burnt-out as I did and that the South Atlantic would finish her off, especially if we met with one of the unpredictable Atlantic bergs the pilot book warned about.

Depending on how long it would take to reach Mar del Plata, the stores should hold. There were MREs for another 33 days. Unfortunately, my Jack Daniel's had dipped to a half-bottle, but there was a quart of Wild Turkey left. The watermaker showed signs of use -- a real concern -- or at least it seemed more difficult to pump. It sapped my waning energy.

My entertainment system was breaking down: My flute

was almost shot, and many of my cassettes, including some of my favorites, would no longer work. Mocking my distrust of gadgets, the GPS continued to function. But everything seemed to be breaking down, including me. I was running on faith.

We were around the Horn, but there were still a number of obstacles in our path. The first was breaking the grip of the powerful Cape Horn current and entering the Falkland current. At all costs, we must avoid the 16-mile-wide Straits of Le Maire between the eastern tip of Tierra del Fuego and Isla de Los Estados.

Dumas warned about this area in which conflicting tides at different times of the day combine with contrary winds to produce seas so violent and choppy, he advised mariners to avoid the entire island by at least 20 miles. I planned to give the island at least that distance on its east side, opposite the Straits.

In doing so, we'd have a chance to avoid the deadly, boiling seas of the overfalls that extend from the east end of the island. They were capable of sinking *Cestus* without a moment's notice.

The trick would be to squeeze through the overfalls on the west and the Burdwood Bank to the east, another violent and choppy region south of the Falkland Islands.

To complicate matters, between the Burdwood Bank and the Falklands lay the Mintay Reef, another deadly obstacle. To avoid disaster, we would have to make a gentle S-shaped course to the north. All the while, we'd be forced to watch for icebergs, which in this part of the Atlantic can extend above 40^0 South latitude.

A few days later, on January 5, I celebrated my 53rd birthday as I was approaching the precarious passage between the overfalls and the Burdwood Bank. I awoke at 5 a.m. to find a freighter of Uruguayian registry off our stern. It had slowed and apparently was scrutinizing us.

In a minute, I was talking via VHF with the master, who identified himself as George. Yes, he said, he would be happy to relay a message to Mary, telling her I had safely rounded the

Horn and was headed home. What a relief it was to send that message. Happy birthday, Frank.

Three hours later, the sun came out and almost gave me an illusion of warmth. I sat in the cockpit, reviewing the past few days, feeling mixed emotions. One was tremendous relief. The other was anxiety, which had grown into an ugly identity of its own since we rounded the Cape.

On the day we rounded the Cape, I had looked south under the layer of high cloud and distinctly saw the sun glittering on the ice pack. Maybe that's when the anxiety began. The bergs that had been vivid phantoms for so long became real and menacing, and I thanked God that every mile we sailed north took us farther from the land of ice. The full gale that pounded us that night generated further anxiety because I had let my guard down slightly, thinking the worst was behind. It was another ordeal of pounding and crashing.

Warnings in the pilot charts induced more anxiety and reinforced Dumas' warnings. I read: "Caution -- Off Cabo San Juan a heavy tide rip extends for a distance of 5 or 6 miles or more to seaward. When the wind is strong and opposed to the tidal current, the overfalls are overwhelming and dangerous; they have been reported to extend 18 miles E of the island. Mariners must use every precaution to avoid this area." Cabo San Juan is the eastern end of Isla de los Estados.

The wind had been dead against us the day before my birthday, and we were trying to overcome a current that was setting us east toward the deadly Burdwood Bank. As I looked back in the late afternoon, I saw an Antarctic storm brewing behind us.

We were beginning the bottom of our S-shaped course, navigating between the overfalls and the Burdwood Bank. My new chart indicated the coast of Argentina is remote. No place looked good for landing in case of emergency.

At least the storm had failed to materialize .

With *Cestus* flying toward Mar del Plata, I routinely bailed the cabin before lunch. While forward, I cracked my temple, but I couldn't feel any blood oozing out from under the tape. Probably a measure of exhaustion, I was making little mistakes in almost everything I did. With several weeks of hard sailing to our destination, that would never do.

To celebrate the day, I enjoyed a meatball dinner, one of my favorite MREs, and a can of tomatoes. I had a merry cocktail hour with a taste of Wild Turkey and glowed with pride in my boat.

The next two days, Friday and Saturday, passed in moderate turmoil. Becalmed and drying out, I constantly changed the sails, trying to maintain my distance from the dangers on both sides. A fog on Saturday added to the irritation of calculating we had covered only 600 miles in 12 days. The frustration set my eyes twitching.

Eating a meager breakfast, I passed time by watching a large shark circle a kelp bed. Behind us, something splashed in the water, but when I turned, only a circle remained.

A station from the Falkland Islands came on the radio, and I enjoyed hearing world news broadcast in English.

We were sailing north, roughly on a line between the Straits of Magellan and the Falklands. And we were sailing handsomely on a broad reach, some of the best sailing of the entire voyage, eating miles. On this side of the South American continent, the seas seemed milder, though some worrisome crosscurrents annoyed us.

Looking forward to re-entering the Forties in the next two or three days, I found an MRE with a rip in the brown bag. At first I hesitated but went on to enjoy it.

Sunday proved an unholy Sabbath. Spasms swept my bowels and I fell deadly ill. In short order, the attack dehydrated me, and I may have become delirious because my log entry read "...Symbolic days. The day of total hot calm with the king of the albatross in the flock. My birthday, George, and turned up. The trots and leaving the 50s, etc."

Monday, a storm struck early in the morning and somehow I managed to get out on deck to heave to, fearing a drift toward Santa Cruz Rock, still to the north toward the mainland. During the day, a definite sign of internal bleeding horrified me. From hour to hour, my strength was crashing.

Too weak to do anything else, I crept into my sleeping bag, where I alternately sweated and shivered. I blazed with fever.

* * * * * * * * * *

The first trigger that sent me voyaging was almost random. I had lived on L dock about three years and had learned to sail by frequent day sailing and cruises to the Channel Islands. I was returning from work one afternoon when I saw one of my neighbors. "Frank, why don't you sail somewhere?" she asked.

She was right. My skills and inclinations suggested a sea voyage far beyond Santa Catalina and a few of the other Channel Islands.

"I am," I said. No doubt, that decision had lurked under my skin for some time. "I'm going to sail the *Boogie* down to Turtle Bay."

That lovely bay about halfway down Baja California in Mexico lay a good 360 miles south of King Harbor.

"Good for you," she said, looking slightly skeptical.

By the time I was back aboard my boat, an iron compulsion gripped me. Now that I said I was going to Turtle Bay, I'd have to do it. It was time I tried my skills and knowledge in a real sea voyage.

When I cast off November 5, 1978, my two companions were Kris, a lovely young lady who loved sailing adventures, and Doug, who had signed on late and was universally known as the Dog-Man because of the quality of his dates.

I thought I had prepared fully, including using a powerful outboard motor for a backup, and had honed my sailing skills, but the *Boogie* was a ship of fools as we sailed out of King Harbor on a brisk November breeze. We began to realize something was amiss when I mistook Mission Bay for San Diego Harbor.

Although we were friends, we soon discovered there wasn't sufficient space -- either physically or psychologically -- for our comfort. A kind of people claustrophobia sailed with us.

We cast off at noon from Mission Bay for our first Mexican port, Ensenada, roughly 70 miles to the south. On the way, we saw a shark that appeared longer than our boat. A minor storm developed, and we had some trouble finding Ensenada. Thinking we had passed it, we turned back. But when I saw a bull ring ashore, I knew we had sailed all the way back to Tijuana, almost back to where we started.

It took 30 hours to reach Ensenada. About 20 of those hours, I was at the helm because the self-steering mechanism refused to function.

Ensenada is a resort for weekend American tourists, who cluster around the harbor, and the home of Mexican citizens, many of whom are trapped by poverty. Traditionally, Americans drink, shop, and often make fools of themselves in Ensenada, the policia keep a semblance of order, the merchants prosper, and everybody is happy, except those trapped by poverty.

Groggily, without wind, we motored out of Ensenada several days later, and down the unmarked, unlighted coast. My crew provided little relief at the helm. Eight days after we had cleared our home port, we anchored in a heavy surge below Punta Colnett, the southernmost area of our first chart. Our strategy was to sail by day and anchor by night whenever possible.

Excitedly, I felt we were deep into the voyage with no turning back. Kris was enjoying the sailing, but the Dog-Man chain-smoked so many Camel cigarettes, he appeared nervous.

The next day, we found good anchorage at the square-mile San Martin Island, about three miles offshore. San Martin is uninhabited, but there was a cluster of cardboard shacks giving evidence that fishermen spent time on the island.

Down to seven gallons of gas, we managed to buy a

good supply from the fishermen and depart for Cedros Island, far to the south. This was my first truly offshore sail. Soon, the worst storm I had experienced to that time struck with 40-knot winds and 12-foot seas.

Besides the storm, my greatest worry was the notorious Sacramento Reef, close in shore and the grief of many an American yachtsman. The reef was strewn with broken boats, and I wasn't sure where it was lurking, waiting to tear out the *Boogie's* hull.

We ran before the wind and a following sea for over 24 hours. At one time, the Dog-Man took the helm but a 12-foot wave broke into the cockpit and we almost broached. After we sailed a day, a night, and a day, my celestial navigation was about 20 miles off, but Kris saw a cloud bank.

"Don't clouds hang around islands?" she said.

It was worth a try. She was correct and we safely anchored after dark on a mud bottom about 35 feet deep at the village on the southeast end of Cedros.

A few days later, we celebrated Thanksgiving aboard by eating abalone with some new acquaintances from a nearby boat. We all had more to drink than we should have, but we thoroughly enjoyed the day. Kris slept aboard with our new friends, giving the Dog-Man and me a little more space for the night.

The next morning, however, Kris announced that she had enough of life confined with Doug and me aboard the *Boogie*. Though the village of Puerto San Bartolome was no metropolis, it did have a small airfield and Kris found a telephone. She called a friend, who flew to Mexico in his light airplane to return her to the States.

When it was time to start home, I decided to dead reckon our way. I estimated our position by our compass course, speed, and elapsed time.

As a result of dead reckoning, a comedy of errors began to play itself out. According to my navigation, we made landfall at Punta San Carlos, but we were actually about seven miles south at Punta Bluff.

When we weighed anchor the next day and sailed north, and we anchored at Punta San Antonio at night, thinking we were at Punta Fernando, still a distance from the legendary Sacramento Reef. The next morning, full of confidence, we rounded the point to see San Jeronimo Island, the marker for the deadly reef.

Mexican fishermen in skiffs yelled and gestured to us, and suddenly I realized that we had to squeeze between the rocks of the Sacramento Reef and the surf line ashore. True to its heritage as an outboard, the motor chose that time to falter. But only momentarily.

I felt the *Boogie's* keel graze the sand. We made it, barely, and I never trusted dead reckoning again.

Then began a slogging against the wind and seas up the coast of the Baja. December definitely was not the time to make this passage. The heavy conditions horrified Doug, and to this day I admire his courage for conquering his terror and sticking with me. At last we reached Ensenada, where I expected Doug to hitch a ride home, but instead he stayed, buying drinks for every bar lady in town. When we finished the trip, I decided that any future ocean voyages would be made without a crew.

After I returned to L dock on the day before Christmas, the Baja voyage was a hot topic of conversation. The second trigger for a major voyage was as simple and random as the first. One of the L dock residents asked conversationally, "Where you sailing next, Frank?"

"Hawaii," I responded, and the same headlong feeling of absolute commitment engulfed me.

Chapter Sixteen

Struggling Up
The Atlantic

My fever had subsided and we had successfully dodged the overfalls by clipping the western edge of the Burdwood Bank. Turning to the northwest, we avoided the Mintay Reef, but in doing so came dangerously close to the Aguila Reef.

All the conditions opposed sailing north along the Argentine coast toward Mar del Plata, located on the south side of the vast mouth of the Rio del Plata. At that point, the river divides Argentina from Uruguay.

From day 110 to day 117, we sailed from 49° 29.7' South latitude 64° 37.3' West longitude to 43° 14.4' South to 59° 37.6' West. Averaging about 55 miles per day, the going was agonizingly slow -- either calms or the wind in our face. I desperately wanted the voyage to end.

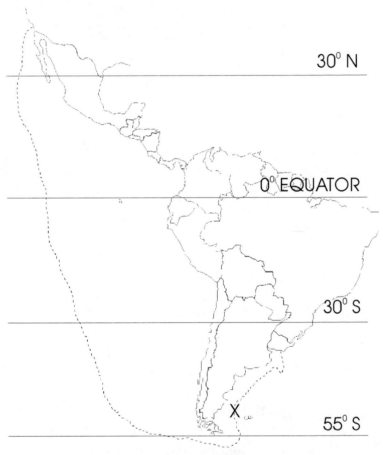

Day 110

January 10, a Tuesday. I was still deathly ill. This was the third day and I felt weak and dehydrated. None of my self-medication helped.

We had already accomplished our main goal, rounding Cape Stiff. In a weird way, the secondary goal, survival, was taking on less importance. The wind was from the exact direction we wanted to sail, and we were in a sector in which my pilot book advised the wind might blow from the north for days at a time.

Cestus chomped at the current dead against her. After pounding all day, changing the sail five times, and the vane now groaning along with the rudder post, *Cestus* virtually stopped at sunset when the wind dropped. For the second night in a row, the South Atlantic becalmed us. We had made a scant 120 miles in three days.

It seemed anything that could go wrong did go wrong. The calm claimed the next day, too, a nightmarish return of the calms we experienced in the Pacific. That seemed like 79 years ago, rather than 79 days. The boat rocked violently in the collage of currents.

We desperately needed headway because we were close to the region where the Falkland current branches off and heads across the Atlantic toward Africa. If we got caught in a trans-Atlantic drift, I'd probably starve.

But whatever my worries, the dawn heralded a most wonderful day because, for the first time in an eon, it seemed, I was warm. I sat in the cockpit, feeling the sun on my head and bare arms. Deep down, my chest absorbed warmth, and my fingers and toes rejoined me. The sun was healing and, despite my infirmities, my mood elevated for the first time since eating the torn MRE.

That night, the wind came up but swirled from all points of the compass. It would blow and stop, blow and stop. Spurred by the prospect of the threatening current, I spent much of the night trying for the proper combination of sails.

Thursday, day 112, heartened me. Apparently we had escaped the east-setting current during the night and, almost as good, my self-medication was beginning to work and my insides felt stable for the first time in days. Almost immediately, I longed for a home-cooked meal, prepared by my darling Mary, served on white linen with our best china and silverware. In our own home. With a glass of wine, and a blue sky clearly visible over King Harbor. Home in a safe port at last.

There was little wind, but again I savored the warmth. I estimated we were 650 miles from Mar del Plata.

I tried to look upon Friday the 13th as a lucky day. In about a 7-knot wind, we were ghosting in the direction of our desired port. That was lucky. The wind came up in the late afternoon, at first to my satisfaction, but by evening, a full gale blew in our teeth.

As always in gale and storm, I feared for the boat. How much longer could it survive, where was the limit to fiberglass? With *Cestus* running under bare poles, I again braced myself between the quarter berths. This was too grim, more than I could stand.

* * * * * * * * * *

As *Cestus* and I ran in the gale, the wonderfully warm passage to Hawaii stole into my consciousness. The day before Christmas 1978, I had written in my diary "... I now commit to sail to Hawaii by November 1980." I vowed this time -- unlike my Baja cruise -- I would do it right: well-prepared and alone. No more crew problems.

Soon after, I met Mary. She agreed I should go, and promised to meet me in Maui.

Hawaii required commitment. This voyage was much more demanding than coasting down the Baja and back. And each following voyage demanded a more powerful commitment than the last until I committed to Cape Horn.

For the voyage to Hawaii, there was serious provisioning. It was canned goods all the way. Although I lacked refrigeration, I didn't overlook a case of warm beer. Tearing out the vee berth, I installed water bladders. At the time, I didn't know that the bulkheads I removed were structurally important. This caused the hull to flex too much and gave me other trouble later. But all the time I was learning valuable skills.

Three days before my departure, Bruce Lane inadvertently crashed into the *Boogie* in its slip. The collision bent my self-steering mechanism, but luckily I was able to tweak it back into shape.

The *Boogie* was full-keeled and its fiberglass well laid-up. Though it had cruised the coast of Southern California and northern Mexico, this would be its first ocean crossing. The *Boogie* would convince me that full-keeled, well laid-up fiberglass boats need not be brand new to make ambitious ocean crossings.

I was 38 and had been sailing 11 years. The *Boogie* was 16 years old.

On June 1, 1980, I cast off, alone and well-prepared aboard the *Boogie*.

Navigating by sextant and noon sights for the first time, I started keeping a log as well as a sea diary. By noon, my body and mind entered the rhythm of the Pacific Ocean, lulling me into a warm cocoon of rolling sea and a dome-like sky. The *Boogie* made itself known to me much more intimately than it ever had on the cruise down the coast of Baja, where other humans intruded. Slowly I grew accustomed to the groaning as the hull flexed.

Hardly had my sea legs developed, when a swift U.S. Navy aircraft carrier almost ran me down. It passed my stern before I realized it was there. I felt it had turned to miss me. Good for the Navy. Otherwise, my ship and I probably would have been destroyed by churning props. From that point on, I was up every half hour all night long. My fatigue grew daily for the remaining 20 days of the voyage.

Before I could brood about my close call, a threat developed that concerns all sensible sailors -- a hurricane. Listening to my time-cube radio, I discovered a tropical storm was turning into a hurricane about 1,000 miles south and 1,000 miles east of me. It gradually swung around in my path. It became known as Hurricane Agatha.

By June 9, Agatha stalked me, advancing straight toward me. Soon I was running before large seas at 25 knots. By Friday, June 13, Agatha was closing and moving at 17 knots toward our rendezvous. Thankfully, its winds had fallen below 100 knots. If everything stayed constant, it should pass behind me by 100 miles.

The seas grew mountainous and challenged the *Boogie's* will to survive. As we constantly surfed downward, I huddled inside the cabin, listening to the hull's working and groaning. It was like continually rising and falling over a cliff, day after day after day and into the nights. As I waited for the final violence, I wished I had a friend aboard.

But the gods smiled, and dying Agatha missed us by almost 100 miles. The *Boogie* survived the huge seas.

Then I wounded myself. For me, woodworking is soothing, especially when I make something useful. I was making a grate for the cockpit sole with a hammer and chisel when the chisel slipped and I pounded a crimson gap between my left thumb and forefinger. I missed the artery by a hair. Tape barely managed to stop the bleeding. As I healed, my self-reliance grew.

On June 26, 1980, I sighted the volcano on Maui, my first, thrilling landfall on an ocean passage. I was elated, deeply satisfied that my navigation had worked. In fact, Hawaii didn't seem hard to find. My provisions had lasted. Most of all, I felt the sweet triumph of basic survival, the magic passage of my body over thousands of miles of ancient ocean canyons, safely, all the way from California.

But safety was a deception. As I approached Maui, I realized the illusion I thought was Maui and Molokai was caused by the Isthmus of Maui. From a distance, it appeared to be two islands. Then when Molokai emerged gray in the distance, I knew I was over the Spartan Reef. Any moment, the reef might slice the hull. Pounding up the lee shore of Maui, ultimately to run through the Pailolo Channel, was heavy sailing, but I escaped the reef.

At last, on June 27, a local hailed me and referred me to a mooring in Lahaina. Without wind, I drifted to it.

I called Mary, who was waiting on the other side of the island. Though it was a joy to be reunited with her, I sadly reflected on brave Mike King. I last saw him in the "Waterworks" bar on Maui three years earlier. He had been diving for black coral in deep water and incurred an injury from the bends. Mike died shortly after our meeting.

Relaxed in the islands, I reflected on the lessons the crossing had taught me. Ocean passages, like everything else, require commitment. Stout old boats, provisioned properly, can cross oceans. My navigation scheme worked up to this point. Safety from collision at sea requires vigilance. The power of the sea, for all practical purposes, is infinite. Re-entry into society is a trial. But the wonderful, positive, congratulatory reaction of friends is almost worth the peril of voyaging.

Reality finally set in. Mary and I had to get back to work.

* * * * * * * * * *

Saturday, January 14, was a vast improvement over the "unlucky day." We had survived another gale. I took advantage of our luck and spent much of the day trying to repair the running lights. Most likely, we would encounter traffic on this leg of the voyage, and being run down at night would be a shameful end.

The batteries had run down and, even after the repairs, the running lights were dim and effective at short range only. After the repair, I pumped a large amount of water from the bilge, but now the accumulation ceased to be threatening.

The warmth had returned to my bones. With good fortune, I would never be cold again. Already I could anticipate the pleasures of Mar del Plata. After taking care of all the bureaucratic aspects of landing, I would stand under a hot shower for 30 minutes.

What a strange feeling it would be to come in after this voyage. The aftermath of my voyage to Japan seemed somewhat bizarre, and that voyage totaled only 87 days at sea. How much more surreal this arrival would be.

In anticipation, I examined a chart of the Mar del Plata area. A rectangle delineated by a broken red line extended about 90 miles to the east of my port and about 35 miles to the south. This was an area to be avoided at all costs -- submarine training operations. South of the dangerous rectangle were areas charted as "unexploded ordnance." Mines left over from the Falkland war? I was just too tired to think about it.

After 114 days, the sails were beginning to show signs of wear. Although they had taken a terrific beating, they had many miles left in them. Ed Taylor and his crew of sailmakers should be proud of their work.

Maybe it was because I was alone for so long or because I had been part of nature for so long, but when I heard on my short-wave radio that National Hockey League rookies had agreed to a limit of $800,000 in annual salary in their first year, it seemed obscene.

A rising gale took my mind off the inequities of this world. It roared all night and into the next morning. And my stomach ailments returned in full force.

During the night, an alien humming noise awakened me. I came on deck to find thousands of lights engulfing us. Nearby was a huge caterpillar of lights from a fishing fleet.

Though I called on my VHF radio, there was no reply. Later I heard conversation that sounded something like Chinese.

It was difficult to tell for sure, but I counted 60 boats. I imagined each was trailing a net and that the fleet covered a lot of water. Just so they didn't snare *Cestus*. I wished them better luck than I had fishing.

We sailed along amid the haunting lights. By dawn, the fleet was behind us.

It was the dawn of January 16, Mary's birthday. I felt depleted, chilled, dehydrated, weaker, at death's door. I could no longer hold down even water. I found my sea diary and wrote, "Honey I've kind of left you out of this diary and I meant it this time more as a record of events, factual, and not emotional. Anyway, I love you. I'm afraid I'm real sick and now it's a question only if I can make it in. I seem also to be making a lot of mistakes. I'm going to lay down and will it to be better."

The next morning, on day 117, we were hard on the wind but making better progress than in the past week. I found some Imodium among my supplies and hoped it would soothe my pain and keep me alive at least until we reached Mar del Plata. Looking up from a reverie about Mary, I saw a heart-warming sight: the *Nacional Santos*, a Brazilian freighter, was stopped there, observing me. Its captain was a nice guy who expected to reach his destination by January 31. He and his ship were bound for Valpariso, Chile, via the Straits of Magellan.

Being in the company of other humans reminded me that my clothes had been reduced to damp rags and my body, craving a bath, felt as if it were rotting away. But I was greatly heartened by the prospect of sending a message to Mary.

By that night, we were bouncing off waves again. It was impossible to carry any sail in the tempest, and the wind drove us back over the miles we had gained during the day.

Racing The Ice To Cape Horn -- *By Frank Guernsey & Cy Zoerner*

Chapter Seventeen

Falling On A Stanchion

The distance between Cape Horn and Mar del Plata, Argentina, is roughly the distance -- as the crow flies -- between Los Angeles and Vancouver, British Columbia, or between Fort Lauderdale, Florida, and New York City. Even though my trusty GPS continued to function accurately, my brain did not.

The lack of food and sleep, the illness that sapped my strength, and the general weariness and anxiety of a major ocean voyage were taking their toll. My estimates of distance became more distorted by fatigue. And every day that struggled by seemed like another crushing weight placed on my shoulders.

Day 118

I had been on deck since 4 a.m., constantly changing and trimming the sails, desperately trying to coax *Cestus* a few more yards, but the effort was fruitless. We just rocked and rolled lazily.

A fly landed on the port lifeline, a dark speck. It was an amazingly intricate piece of life. How far was it from land? My guess was 180 miles from the Argentine coast. Did it hop from vessel to vessel to arrive aboard *Cestus*? Did a vagrant breeze waft it here?

That was unlikely because of the north wind prevailing for days now. I welcomed my little companion aboard, but when I went below for the video camera, he disappeared.

Disappointed, I took our daily fix: 42° 31.6' South latitude by 58° 49.8' West longitude. Though I was unsure of my estimate, we were about 80 percent of the way from Cape Horn to our destination.

Tacking all day east and west and making little progress toward our goal, we seemed in disfavor with the sea gods. If we didn't move for 17 days, I'd be out of food. There were about three servings of dried fruit remaining and maybe three days of beef jerky. And there were only three remaining shots of Wild Turkey.

Talking aimlessly to the video camera, I wondered if we were going to make it at all. Training the camera on the chart to show my audience the submarine training area near Mar del Plata, I was really reminding myself of the danger at the end of the voyage.

As we drew closer to civilization, once again I brooded over the Good Samaritan who sought a bottle of scotch for his assistance. That was the kind of society we were returning to. Trying to drive the pettiness from my mind, I recalled the lines from the Gnostic Gospel that says, "If you bring forth what is within you, what you bring forth will save you; if you do not bring forth what is within you, what you do not bring forth will destroy you." Maybe this brooding was healthy.

The fact was, I was weary of everything -- weary of being sick, weary of saltwater sores, weary of the hard fiberglass, weary of calms and currents and contrary winds and gales and storms. This wasn't the impossible voyage; it was the interminable voyage.

At 1:30 p.m., thunder boomed across the dark sky, startling me into reefing. Not far behind it, a few bolts of lightning stabbed down in a frightening display of power. Lightning is rare in Southern California, but I knew it tended to strike at highest points, in this instance at the top of the mast.

A cable linked my steering vane to the backstay attached to the top of the mast. This was my lightning arrestor, the theory being that the lightning bolt would follow the backstay to the cable, on to the steering vane, and from there harmlessly into the water. I didn't want to see the idea put into practice. The lightning display, however slight, foretold the full gale that hit us at the end of the day. I recorded a summary in the navigational log: "DAY WAS A BITCH." Still, as I lay in my bunk, I thanked God that I was feeling better physically. The torn MRE was the most likely suspect, but perhaps bacteria had accumulated on improperly cleaned utensils. Whatever, my delicate physical system was returning to balance.

Day 119

The residue of the gale blasted at the double-reefed main and reefed jib. Though I should have shortened sail, we were at last pointing north, and I wanted to take every advantage to get into port. We pounded incessantly and soon either *Cestus* or I would give out.

Falling off the waves, *Cestus* often met another coming up. Bracing myself in the humid cabin, I ruminated on the complex relationship between Mary, the sea, and me.

From the day I met her, I was taken with Mary, and we had a glorious romance. Our first weekend together, we drove my Volkswagen Bug to San Francisco, Mary's former home, on a Friday morning. That night, we joined several of Mary's friends for a night on the town. It was her first outing as a newly single lady, and it was like a whirlwind honeymoon. Sunday morning, we drove down the coast through Big Sur, happy and full of energy and romance.

I persuaded her to move aboard the *Boogie*. We were alike in that we were both recovering from devastated marriages and we both had children.

Mary's children, Wayne and Ligaya, along with Frankie, often spent weekends aboard the boat in a "one big happy family" congregation. Mary would cook wonderful, gourmet breakfasts on the two-burner alcohol stove. I loved the good times. Mary and I were madly in love and she was -- and is -- one of the most alluring ladies I have ever seen.

We were unlike each other, however, in both temperament and cultural background. But for the whole first year together, none of the problems surfaced. Even after problems began to arise, we knew that our love was deep, permanent, and maddening. But when our relationship is profoundly troubled, as it has been from time to time, I cannot bear it, and I must escape to my other love, the sea.

Then a magic thing happens. Mary and I make up, almost as if putting myself deliberately in danger makes me more attractive to her and her even more precious to me.

The state of my relationship with Mary triggered every voyage after Hawaii -- Tahiti, Japan, and Cape Horn. And Mary has flown to meet me at the end of the other voyages. These have been glorious renewed honeymoons, and if *Cestus* and I reached Mar del Plata, Mary would join me there.

Prior to this voyage, my life wasn't going well. Not only were Mary and I separated, but my insurance business was flagging. I was reading George Orwell's *Down and Out in Paris and London,* when I realized I wasn't far from poverty myself. In February 1989, I moved aboard a friend's Challenger, a 24-foot sailboat. People hinted that I was homeless. Even I began to wonder.

At the rate I was going, it wouldn't be long until my

shoes had holes in them. Later, living in a place in Redondo Beach I called "The Dungeon," I became acutely aware of my plight. Most frightening of all, it was easy to picture myself someday dying while trying to sell insurance. Better to commit to a sea adventure.

Day 120

The storm retreated into the morning, leaving only light air and fog. We had made only 125 miles toward Mar del Plata in three days. Even the albatross tribe, so faithful since the other side of Cape Horn, had deserted us. We proved too slow for them, I supposed.

To my video camera, I predicted we would be snug in the harbor within two days. Even while speaking, I knew it was wishful thinking.

"Only one-half shot of booze left," I lamented to the camera, "and I think 13 meals. Those red dots on the charts represent unexploded ordnances, and they bother me. But I'm even more annoyed by running out of the wherewithal for cocktail hours. They've been one of the high points of each day -- sometimes the only high point -- and I'm really going to miss them. Nobody should have to sail without cocktail hour."

I wondered how I'd look in the tapes. All my clothes were in rags, my beard was uncontrolled, and the bash to my temple probably looked hideous.

Day 121

That morning at 10:30, the fishing vessel *Promac* came to take a look at us. He was a far cry from the ominous, gray gunboat. *Promac's* master, Sestio, gave us a warm and friendly hail. He relieved my sourness about re-entering civilization with its credit cards and ATM cards and Social Security cards and all the other cards that ensnare us. A decent human being, Sestio reminded me the world was full of others like him.

Before going about his business, he advised we were between 145 and 150 miles from Mar del Plata and warned that we were close by the mine fields a few miles to the east.

Later, another boat, rusty and flying what looked like the flag of Argentina, checked us out. With all these reminders of returning to the pack, I pumped extra water to wash what was left of my hair.

That evening, after my last drops of the Wild Turkey, my illness returned. Too weak to do anything else, I lay in my bunk and listened to the north wind rise to 25 knots, followed by the sickening din of the mast pumping up and down. Before drifting into a reverie of running on the beach past the Marina Cove apartments, I wondered abstractly if we would strike a mine.

Day 122

After a night of terrible pounding, we had made only 40 miles toward Mar del Plata in 24 hours. Though the wind should have been westerly, it remained from the north, blowing right on our nose.

Relentless pounding throughout the whole day of Monday, January 23, led to a night hove to about 110 miles from our destination. Before falling asleep, I tried to focus on the positive: I was warm. But the slowly approaching submarine area haunted my dreams.

Day 123

Down to almost no food, I had the last dried fruit for breakfast. Just about everything was gone except a few cans. The food situation was growing critical, as critical as reaching port ... now.

As if in answer to my needs, dark clouds formed and the wind backed to the west. Out on deck in the warm wind smelling of the land, I trimmed sail, and we were in for the best reach of the entire voyage. *Cestus* was a rocket.

By 10 a.m., our reach was becoming too splendid. The wind continued to rise. Not wanting to reduce sail after 35-mile days of pounding, I let *Cestus* run.

The seas slacked off, and we were making 6 knots.

Glorious. To celebrate, I ate the last tiny piece of beef jerky. The temperature dropped and, invigorated, I could envision being in port within an hour. The night sky grew darker and lower, and distant thunder rolled across the waters.

Then lightning sputtered down, first in short thrusts and then to the water. The sky lit with strange strobe lights. I started taping to preserve the moment. I had never seen an electrical storm. It was terrifying but magnificent. The storm lasted into the small hours of the next day.

The wind backed farther to the south, and almost immediately the seas began to build. We were sailing north with a vengeance. Soon the following seas were in sets such as the surfers enjoy in Hawaii. I felt their tremendous power as they rose up behind us.

As I reached to alter the sails, I went up and the boat went down. Losing my balance, for an agonizing moment I was suspended in midair. I fell backward, a stanchion almost impaled my ribs, and a flash of white light blossomed in my head.

* * * * * * * * * *

A June 1984, diary entry reads, "Mary and I separated Friday last. Today I have committed to sail to Tahiti this coming June."

Why Tahiti? Across the equator, it seemed a logical progression, farther and more difficult than Hawaii. Again, I had nothing to gain but finding adventure, living life, and making another run.

The February 10, 1985, diary entry reads, "I have acquired (last June) the *Amethyst,* a 24-foot strip-planked sloop. This boat is an Ostkust (Swedish for East Coast), a design created by Al Mason, one of his first." Mason worked for Sparkman and Stevens in the late 1930s.

The *Amethyst* was conceived in 1942, the year of my

birth. The builder, Art Smith, is Welsh, as is my mother. Amethyst is my mother's birthstone. Later I learned that Joshua Slocum once commanded a ship christened the *Amethyst*.

My *Amethyst* -- a fractional-rigged, hand-made boat -- and I were made for each other. Art Smith built it and named it in honor of his brother, who had served aboard a British gunship by that name.

Built of wood, it measured 24 feet, 1 inch on deck. Its waterline -- the highest point the water reaches on the hull -- was 19 feet, 2 inches. The June 1944 *Rudder* magazine described the Ostkust as a "smart, small racing-cruising auxiliary." A master shipwright, Smith spent ten years in its making. After changing hands several times, the *Amethyst* became mine.

It was 15 years old, beautiful, and traditional -- a great boat. I bought her from a Sikh Indian named John whose plans to sail her to India didn't materialize.

To make space, he had stripped it below.

Gone was everything inside the hull except the floorboards with storage underneath. Gone was the engine, gone were the quarter berths, gone were the ribs. Though this bothered some of my friends, the strip-planking was strong without ribs, as the *Amethyst* would prove. The strength of its beams would hold it all together. At my purchase, it was embryonic, a boat, a cavern, and some said a crypt.

Provisioning was more organized after my Hawaii experience. I still have provisioning lists from all my voyages, ever-lengthening "to-do" lists.

Among the few things that came with the *Amethyst* were 5-gallon black jugs, perfect for water. I stowed them below and on deck. The weight topsides made the deck creak so badly that I finally stowed them all below

By the time I departed from King Harbor on April 29, 1985, Mary and I were back together.

Jack Tatum, a good sailor and friend, towed me out with his 38-foot wooden sloop, *Jo Too*, a former Transpac race winner.

Hawaii had been a fun trip. Tahiti was serious. We would cross the equator this time and be forced to contend with the counter-currents. Almost immediately, my SatNav electronic navigation system broke, and once again I was relying on my sextant and tables. The Navy was practice-bombarding San Clemente Island as I passed, and that black and galing night, the main halyard jammed in the block at the masthead. There was nothing to do in 25 knots of wind but climb the mast.

A little more than halfway up in the boatswain's chair, I lost my grip on the mast and began rotating high above the seas like a child's tether ball. My weight made the mast a lever, and at one point, just as I got hold of the mast again, a spreader almost dipped into the water. We had almost capsized.

How amusing to end my voyage this close to home, tossed into the ocean or splattered on deck. This operation was taking all my strength, and I could feel my 43 years. But finally, holding the halyard in my teeth and using both hands and both feet, I managed to clear the jammed line.

It was all a foolish mistake. Later I discovered that it could have been freed from below. Sail and learn. In fact, most of my sailing skills and knowledge comes from such trial-and-error (or terror) at sea.

Already I learned the *Amethyst* was really punishing. Since it had only floorboards, I slept on a mat that I would move from side to side, depending on my tack and the heel of the boat. I kept my clothes in nets, and from dirty clothes I made bean bags to lean against.

On May 10, I noted that in two weeks I'd be where Hurricane Agatha was five years ago. This trip would make dodging Agatha child's play. Force 7 (28-33 knots of wind) is the practical limit for boats up to 40 feet long. The *Amethyst* was 24 feet, and on our way to Tahiti we would encounter three gales of Force 8 (34-40 knots), and three shorter squalls of about the same wind intensity.

Nine days after I swung around the mast off San

Clemente Island, a full gale struck. The next day, May 11, squalls bent us over, followed by a day of gentle trade-wind sailing. Another full gale slammed us on May 17. More squalls on May 22, and then on June 1, we crossed the equator for the first time. Soon the equatorial counter-currents vexed us. It was my first experience with them. On June 3, we were triple-reefed and screaming in 35 knots. Then the weather moderated and we found ourselves sailing among the dolphins.

For the first time, I was reading *Alone Through the Roaring Forties* by Vito Dumas. It is an account of his circumnavigation in 1942. Perhaps that stout Argentinean planted Cape Horn seeds in the back of my mind. Further reading disclosed a warning on the EPIRB -- the automatic emergency radio transmitter that broadcasts a distress signal and location -- to replace the battery by 1984. It was a year past its limit. Never again did I carry an EPIRB.

On this voyage, I found peace of mind only ten days out. For the first time I looked at a Bible, and I began reading the New Testament. I continued each day so that I could finish it before arriving. For some reason, sunsets, my favorite time of day, produced a profound spiritual feeling. It was the beginning of a sea-inspired spirituality that deepened with my later voyages.

During this trip I started another habit that continued: playing the recorder and later the flute. After my disastrous woodworking experience, I decided to amuse myself in a safer way. I bought a recorder with an instruction book. The recorder is wooden, an early form of the flute with eight finger holes. Although I later took lessons, I confined my flute playing to times at sea.

Avoiding the coral and the islands of the Marquesas and the reefs of the Tuamotus, tested my navigation. Then late one afternoon toward cocktail hour while awaiting the treat of sunset and enjoying my shot of brandy, I looked out across the translucent sea. There stood a sharp, lethal-looking dorsal fin. The surface pulsed.

The shark, a huge, primitive, graceful eating machine, took an interest in me. At 16 feet, it was more than 65 percent the length of my craft. For the next two hours, I watched fascinated as the monster prowled along after me, first to port, then starboard, then dropping aft only to advance again.

June 7 provided another sobering experience. A mile away, a yellow man-overboard pole bobbed dismally in the water. Though I didn't want to, I tacked, not knowing what to expect, sharks eating a half-alive body? Yet I felt bound to check it out.

There was no human. Only the pole, striking me with cold terror. There is no finding anyone in this ocean.

Late afternoon several days later, a glorious landfall. Riding the bow looking for it, I sighted Huahine from about 25 miles off, just where I thought it would be. I was elated that my sextant navigation held good.

It would take two more days before I was safely anchored because of my 1869 French survey chart. I saw the airport and that the island was inhabited all around, but of course none of this was charted and I didn't know where to come in. Fishermen misdirected me and soon the venturi between Moorea and Tahiti caught me. The wind from a driving thunderstorm blew me down channel. Luckily, a cigarette boat, a fast and powerful motorboat, was cavorting up and down the channel and the skipper saw I was in distress and guided me in.

Once I got inside the reef, the wind died and I couldn't get the sails up in time to avoid crashing into the docks. Sailboats come with huge cargoes of humility. A French couple towed me to Maeva Beach, where I anchored just below the airport in Papeete. It was June 15, 1985. I had been 47 days at sea, counting the day between King Harbor and Avalon.

I called Mary, who flew down to join me. My plan was to hire a captain to sail the *Amethyst* home, but it was hurricane season. Finally I found Casey Brooks, who offered to sail it back. He needed the money and I needed to resume my business. On a handshake, he agreed to deliver the boat to me with the option of terminating in Hawaii if the voyage went badly, and I flew home to California.

It did and he did. I flew to Hawaii, relieved Brooks, and provisioned the boat. Unfortunately, nobody warned me about leaving when I did because I drifted onto the coral right in front of the entrance to Ale Wai Harbor near Waikiki Beach.

While the *Amethyst* ground her hull on the coral, everyone ignored my pleas except one man. He swam out, stood on the razor-sharp coral -- where I watched his feet bleed into the clear water -- and pushed me off. My thanks to him. Eventually I got a tow into a boatyard to repair the hull.

Soon after, I met an old gentleman who wanted to sail my sloop to Redondo Beach. My problems solved, I flew home. I never saw him again. A month later, he called to say he got only as far as the nearest point of land.

I called the Matson Line. Boats on trailers were being shipped back from the Transpac race. Yes, the *Amethyst* could join them. She arrived in Alameda Bay. When a friend and I met her with his jeep, we discovered that someone had broken into poor *Amethyst*. She was filthy and empty. Anything worth stealing was gone, sextants and all.

The Tahiti trip reconfirmed all the lessons Hawaii had taught me. Basking in the good wishes of friends and relatives, I counted the additional lessons Tahiti taught: Planning pays in effectiveness. Perseverance pays in results. Experience pays in confidence and skills. Confidence pays, among other things, in sleep aboard. Long voyages pay in peace of mind, the loss of destructive shoreside emotions.

But most of all Hawaii and Tahiti -- 74 days alone at sea -- confirmed that I am a single-hander. In the future, I would always seek my own company for major sea adventures. What I didn't learn was how soon again I'd commit to another longer, more challenging, and more dangerous path, to the next step in my evolution as a single-hander -- Japan.

Chapter Eighteen

Missing A Safe Port

How many days are left to me, I wondered. I lay in my berth feeling as if a harpoon had dug four inches into my back. There was no question that the stanchion had caused internal damage and I needed immediate medical attention. I could hardly get my breath. Each movement of the boat caused renewed pain. I was sure I had bruised something, possibly a kidney.

Day 124
Despite my injury, we needed to get to Mar del Plata.

My ribs were almost too painful for me to move and we self-steered toward our goal. Only the excitement of ending the voyage kept me going. We were close enough that I should be manning the tiller, keeping watch for surfacing foreign submarines and praying that none surfaced under us. But the pain prevented me from even lifting anything.

By 8 a.m., we were on the exact latitude of Mar del Plata, but too far to the east. To make matters worse, the boat pounded into the wind and current in a rising gale from the west, and we were being blown back and out to sea. Painfully mounting the deck to heave to, I could see the buildings of Mar del Plata not 12 miles away.

I needed help desperately. The direction of the wind and current, combined with my physical vulnerability, made sailing into the harbor impossible. Even with a stout outboard engine, entry would have been difficult. The Atlantic fought us all the way and it was about to win.

There was practically no food left, and my injured back might prohibit working the watermaker. Trying to sit upright in the cockpit, I yielded and, holding the VHF radio close to my lips, I called Mar del Plata in a desperate voice.

"This is the sailing vessel *Cestus* ..."

No response.

"This is the sailing vessel *Cestus* calling Mar del Plata for assistance. Over."

Silence. We were being swept back into the submarine practice area. Perhaps the Coast Guard at Mar del Plata didn't speak English.

I tried calling in my restricted Spanish. Still no response. I could not bring myself to utter "Mayday."

My only chance to save myself was to outsmart the gale by clawing our way north of the port and then trying to tack southwest back to it. In that attempt, only I will know the punishment *Cestus* took. The wind howled and the seas broke against us. We tried reversing our tactics and struggling northwest to make west.

By 9 a.m., I had raised a patch of the main and the storm jib right in the teeth of the gale. I was gaining confidence that even if we could not fight our way into Mar del Plata during the blow, we might hold our own and make it into port when the wind and seas subsided. The gale couldn't last forever.

I prayed the gale would by some miracle clock around to the east and blow me straight into port. The ache in my ribs was almost unbearable.

The spindrift showered in my face, but at least it was warm. As the hours passed, I grew weaker, lightheaded. Engaging Leo to steer, I went below for some stale crackers to generate energy. It dawned on me that the disappearance of the albatross tribe probably meant no more than that I had quit sharing crackers with them.

In my sea diary, I recorded "... can't last much longer. This must be the final run."

Back in the cockpit, I saw we had lost some ground. Mar del Plata was the most elusive port we had ever tried to gain. Wild thoughts visited me. I felt like giving up and going with the flow all the way to Africa.

With the spray stinging my eyes and my back throbbing, I retreated into a memory of one of the trips Mary and I took to San Francisco to visit her friends, in those sweet days shortly after we married in 1982.

We were cruising up Highway 1 in our Lincoln. We felt playful, running free through Big Sur. We had shed part of our clothing to enjoy the sunshine, food and drink when we got trapped behind a bus full of Japanese tourists. Because of the winding road, we had no chance to pass for almost an hour.

Instead of watching the beautiful, mountainous terrain, the tourists crowded to the back of the bus and watched us. They laughed and waved cheerily while we waved back and toasted them. Before long, we became their photo subjects, and Mary and I laughed about how these tourists would need photographic evidence to prove to their countrymen that Americans really are as fun-loving as reputed.

215

These happy days fled like the horizon at sea. In 1986, Mary and I separated. At 44, I felt bereft, moved back aboard my boat, and committed to sail to Japan, certainly the longest and most dangerous ocean passage to that date.

Thank God, we reunited the next year and, to celebrate, we treated ourselves to a second honeymoon in Paris. Nothing could have pleased me more than having Mary back before sailing to Japan. September in Europe was a romantic interlude. We stayed in the Latin Quarter, and ate and drank in the sidewalk cafes in the cool, brilliant sunshine.

The French culture embraced us, and our spirits soared as our love reasserted itself. At times like that -- in love in Paris -- it seemed impossible we ever quarreled.

We returned to the States, and once again Mary understood my compulsion to honor my commitment to the Japan voyage.

The torture in my back brought me back to reality. The pain increased like a growing flame as the hours wore on. The gale showed no intent of subsiding. Six hours of struggling toward the harbor was all I could bear. At 7 p.m., I made the heartbreaking decision to turn away and try for Uruguay. In every other danger of the voyage, I had desperately wanted to live. This time, I hardly cared. Perhaps we could reach Punta del Este, across the huge and treacherous mouth of the Rio del Plata.

Carefully, I brought *Cestus* about and set Leo to steer us in a northerly direction. I wasn't sure where we were going, but perhaps Montevideo or Punta del Este, Uruguay, would provide a haven.

I spread a chart across my knees in the cabin. Whatever the future held, we were on our last chart. The 38th parallel of south latitude bisects Mar del Plata. The 35th parallel runs just south of Punta del Este and Montevideo, so roughly speaking, though little remained of our supplies and endurance, we had 180 sea miles to go. If conditions didn't improve, that could add five or six days to the voyage. In ideal conditions, we could make it in two days. So would it be Montevideo or Punta del Este?

Montevideo seemed the more hazardous choice. Banco Rouen, Banco Arquimedes, and Banco Ingles stood between us and the Uruguayan capital. The bottom of the river mouth was strewn with shipwrecks, and we had no desire to join them. We had already had enough of treacherous waters. Punta del Este, on the other hand, appeared the safer way, the chief hazard being Banco Rouen, which we could keep well to port. Fifty-five degrees West longitude practically splits Punta del Este. We would have to stay west of that line, lest the current sweep us up the Uruguyan coast into oblivion.

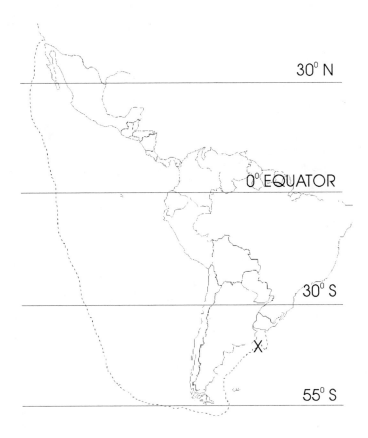

Punta del Este it would be. I wearily set Leo to steer us at 26^0 true.

* * * * * * * * * *

"I have discovered that the way of the Samurai is death. In a 50/50 life or death crisis, simply settle it by choosing immediate death. There is nothing complicated about it. Just brace yourself and proceed. One who chooses to go on living having failed in one's mission will be despised as a coward and a bungler. In order to be a perfect Samurai, it is necessary to prepare one's self for death, morning and evening, day in and day out."

These words of Yukio Mishima summarize my fascination with a culture like Japan's. I admire people who can say things like that about their spirit and way of life. So when my relationship with Mary struck on the shoals a year after returning from Tahiti, Japan seemed like a logical destination.

July 3, 1986, I committed to sail to the island of Honshu no later than April 1988. I planned to sail nonstop to Tokyo or Kobe, near Osaka. My boat was now 18 years old, and its master was 46.

By this time, the good early days on L dock were in the past. I understood that ocean crossings demand a certain sobriety and seriousness of purpose.

During a record-breaking local heat wave, I set sail from King Harbor on Friday, March 25, 1988. Even though Mary and I had reunited before the voyage, my departure was a somber one, almost morbid, in fact. It was true that Japan would be tough, uphill slugging, but as I embarked I felt the familiar primitive excitement in the pit of my stomach.

Nine days after embarking from Avalon, I rammed a log, a big mossy devil, which at first appeared to cause no damage. Sixteen days later, however, the *Amethyst* was leaking. Not severely, but sea water sloshed in the bilge, and when she rolled, it welled up through the floorboards and drenched my makeshift bunk. I discovered the planks forward were weeping in the area where the former owner had removed the ribs and where we hit the log.

Later, a squall hit, and I went out to douse the jib. Squinting through the blown spume, I saw a hole in the sail. As I yanked it down on the bucking deck, the shackle came undone, and the halyard shot up the mast. My stomach sank. It was like my fiasco on the Tahiti trip. There was no escaping another wild, slapstick climb.

Again, halfway up I lost hold, and the swinging mast whipped me around. The only difference was that this time I was up the mast in a trade-wind squall, the boatswain's chair under my armpits, the sloop rolling terribly with my weight up top. By late afternoon, all was under control, but I was exhausted and badly scratched. So much for the learning curve.

More problems followed. On April 22, 200 miles out of Hilo, Hawaii, the vane broke completely. After that, I was chained to the helm, slumped in the cockpit in the sun and wind and under the stars, trying to sail the boat. A wild jibe slashed the main sheet across my face.

Bitterly disappointed, I had no choice but to steer for the nearest land, the big island of Hawaii. My ambition to sail nonstop to Japan died in anguish. On April 25, we were in Radio Bay, Port Hilo, tied up Tahiti style, stern to shore.

Two days later, Mary arrived to enjoy Hawaii with me and stayed until repairs were complete.

On Tuesday, May 3, I again set sail, but in short order the vane broke. The next morning, I was back in Radio Bay, more exasperated than at my first arrival. But by this time, I was getting the hang of the vane, and nine days later I secured it and cast off again.

I was jubilant to be at sea again after the 18-day delay and to be once again sailing for Japan. Soon afterward, birds warned of a shoal dead ahead, and they served a stern warning. My celestial navigation would have to be heads up. Nature had sprinkled the ocean with obstacles -- reefs, submerged volcanic cones -- waiting to destroy us. The strategy for avoiding them was a nautical chess game. Deciding to stay 3^0, or 180 miles, north of Rional Reef and Rene Reef, I planned to follow an average of 22^0 North latitude.

I would pass Wake Island to port and then work up to 23^0 North latitude and pass just under the first Japanese island, Minami-tori Shima, at approximately 24^0 North latitude and 154^0 East longitude. Then, as I turned North, I'd run the gauntlet through a string of Volcanic Islands that waited to claim me and my *Amethyst*. The first group would be the Kazan Retto, the next the Ogasawara Gunto, then up through the Nampo Shoto.

At this time I checked my water supply. The black jugs had sailed with me thousands of miles to Tahiti and now toward Japan. They were among the few things that came with the *Amethyst*. For the first time I noticed embossed lettering on the plastic. "May be hazardous when empty. Container is not reusable for food or drinking substances." That "drinking substances" included water seemed clear. It was too late now. Alone, far offshore, I enjoyed the irony.

My planned landfall would be Hachijo Jima, an island in the Izu Shoto Group. I'd follow that group to Sagami Bay, where I'd find the entrance to Tokyo Bay, marked by the island of Oshima. The sea, of course, can have its own plans. Humans propose, the sea disposes.

I came on deck to have a look. Directly astern, a junk was closing in light air. If I hadn't looked at that moment, the junk would have overtaken me.

It was over a 100 feet long, and it looked as if there were about 50 people crowded aboard. Its ominous, dark hull dogged me. He called on his VHF, but I couldn't understand what I thought to be Vietnamese. Apparently, he didn't hear my response, though my radio had been working in Hilo. He kept talking, but because I heard no "Mayday" and the junk, in fact, was sailing in hot pursuit, I felt no obligation to slow. Instead, I broke out the 30-06 rifle and tacked up into the little weather there was.

He tacked.

I tacked again.

He tacked. It became a duel as if we were in a Tuesday night race at the Redondo Beach Yacht Club's Horizon Series. But this wasn't innocent club racing. Luckily, he had no engine. It turned out the *Amethyst* could point higher in light air, sail at a closer angle to the wind. All night I stayed anxiously at the helm, and first light revealed that I had lost him, never to see him again. After evading the would-be pirate, we ghosted safely past Minami-tori Shima.

After we evaded the obstacles and turned up toward Japan, "the insane storm from nowhere," as I called it in my sea diary, struck. It was the most frightening to date, followed by more storms and gales. As they smashed us, my provisions neared zero. I ate my last mushy apple, and worse, I was down to the last of the toilet paper.

As the seas came up and as I hove to, I discovered there was a typhoon to the west approaching me on a collision course. For a week I sailed on the heavy weather. The wind climbed to 50 knots, but the heart of the typhoon missed us.

The wind stopped on July 3, leaving me powerless in the mounting ship traffic. I thanked God that we weren't racing along because my generator line snagged a big red buoy that held fishing nets. If I had been sailing at speed, that buoy could have ripped out our transom.

July 5 found me up all night in the shipping lanes with a flashlight on the sails. Despite my efforts, the solar panels and generator failed to produce enough juice to keep my running lights glowing. At 2 p.m., I thrilled to another landfall, the land of the Samurai. It was the island of Miyake Jima.

That night, it was flashlight on the sails again, and six freighters, their engines pounding in the dark, turned to miss me at the entrance to Tokyo Bay. The next morning, I thought I was at the Island of Oshima, but it was the entrance to Sagami Bay.

Current against me, I entered Sagami Bay on Thursday, July 7, and the traffic was terrific. Again, my trusty flashlight illuminated the sails and protected me from being run down. In the morning, a flotilla of tugs headed out. The city to my left was Ito, and the entrance to Tokyo bay was to my right. I was becalmed, inching toward land.

A fishing boat chugged out and towed me into Ito.

Safely docked, I was feeling happy and fulfilled. A newspaper reporter came by, and I locked the boat and followed him -- still on sea legs -- to his office about two blocks away in the crowded little city. In the busy newspaper building, I called Mary, a $50 toll, and the call was on the house. It looked as if I'd get the celebrity treatment.

Then the police came.

I wasn't afraid, but for some reason, the police appeared uncomfortable. After 57 days at sea, I suppose my looks would have frightened anyone. My mild mood persisted as they escorted me to the police station. I decided to be polite. The station looked like bureaucratic headquarters anywhere with cream and pea green walls, dark linoleum floors, and scarred furniture. Quite formally, fifteen officers arranged themselves in a semi-circle around me. What was this all about? I couldn't understand a word, even though they seemed to be questioning me. Throughout, one officer smiled.

Soon an interpreter arrived. A mild-mannered fellow, he too seemed uncomfortable, almost frightened, adding to my relaxed confusion. I made out from him that certain phone calls were being made about me to Yokohama, Yokosuka, and other naval and Coast Guard centers. I suppose the police didn't know what to do with me. What an odd, almost funny, welcome. It seemed to bother them that their reception didn't bother me.

In the early morning of July 8, the police reached a decision. The interpreter told me that I had to go to Misakiko, a port of entry across the bay, and take my boat with me. Now that was more easily said than done because I had no idea where Misakiko was. The traffic in the bay was deadly and the currents were contrary. Besides, the visibility was equal to cotton. It hardly mattered that I had no proper charts.

Kicked off my mooring at 5 a.m., I was to be awake for the next 36 hours in a kind of surrealistic sailing nightmare. My carefree mood had vanished. As I crossed Sagami Bay in a heavy fog, a large shark stalked me. Was it the garbage in the bay or me it wanted? That night as I was hove to offshore, the lights on land and on passing vessels confused me.

By daylight, I saw land, but I steered the wrong way and headed toward Hayama into an area where the Japanese submarines practice with wooden torpedoes. Being sunk by a wooden torpedo would be an inglorious end to my voyage.

At last realizing my error, I turned back, and I ducked into and out of four small harbors, all the wrong ones. The wind and seas climbed, driving me shoreward, and I almost lost it all. Clawing out to sea, I survived this hazard. I was beating up the shoreline when I was set down on a reef about a half-mile long.

To quote my log, "... I approached and I was finally committed and I couldn't then fall off or tack out as I kept coming. This was the moment of truth in my life. I kept coming and chanced it... I eventually was no more than 30 yards out and in the surf line -- 30 plus knots of wind and too much sail up, but couldn't now leave the tiller for fear of losing any ground and at the toss of the coin; dear Amethyst beat along and finally looked to pass the danger and we did."

How I managed to beat away from that menace, I'll never know. It was many minutes before my heart quit beating wildly.

Soon afterward, I thought we were there. I was now living on remaining granola dust. I tried several entrances in heavy swells and light wind. Once I almost went up the boat ramp at a boat yard. Unbelievably, I managed to tack and beat out, missing a fleet of alarmed fishing dinghies.

At last, bone weary and confused, I spotted a beautiful, big American yacht, the *Diablesse*, with a crew of seven, and hailed her. When I asked for Misakiko, he called out, "You're here and follow me." We followed it into Aburatsubo Harbor, beautiful with a lush, green shoreline, arriving just after noon.

223

There I met Fukotome, who owns and manages a small section of the harbor. He is one of the foremost sailing authorities in Japan and rigs many top racing yachts. This gracious man befriended me.

So did the Japanese media corps. In one day, seven reporters visited me. Fifteen minutes of fame embarrassed me and I couldn't even read the press accounts, but I feared the worst. Neither did I see the television interviews, but I feared the worst there, too.

After the journalists came the quarantine people, the customs, and the Coast Guard. Three policemen arrived and took my rifle. They counted the bullets and fired the weapon once before returning it to me. Then immigration visited as I was still drying out and finishing the last of the videotape that I made for the first time during a voyage. I was told that sailors didn't cross Sagami Bay without engine or electronics. Good advice, but too late.

More problems of the land engulfed me. I was impoverished. One pair of jeans on Fukotome's clothesline, $100, a Mastercard, a little money somebody gave me, and my *Amethyst* were my entire estate. I'd eventually be forced to sell her for $3,500 to a local, a retired sergeant, who planned to sail her around the world.

On July 12, I left the *Amethyst* under the care of friends in Aburatsubo and took the train about 60 miles to Tokyo and met Mary. My credit card produced money from a local bank so that Mary and I could tour parts of Japan. I loved Japan for its beauty, the Japanese for their manners, helpfulness, and efficiency. Though to some people Tokyo seems too crowded, it delighted me.

The voyage to Japan reconfirmed the lessons of Hawaii and Tahiti. Commitment. A basically seaworthy boat. Planning. Careful preparation. Proper provisions. Navigational skills. Vigilance. Fortitude. Deep respect for the sea. Sea time. The pangs of re-entry. And, of course, good luck, a requirement for a safe crossing.

Chapter Nineteen

Arriving In Uruguay

The first time I heard the expression "Do or die," I was in Mrs. Sullivan's School. When one of my classmates shouted it in a game, it struck me as the most dramatic utterance possible. As the years wore on and I heard it applied to trivial situations, it became dull, cliche. But now *Cestus* and I were in a situation in which its meaning was clear and true. If we didn't make Punta del Este, we would die.

Because each day extracted a high toll in stamina, now was the time to give everything, to use every last drop of adrenaline, to sustain my resolve for life, to make the final mental and physical effort to save myself.

Day 125

My Triumph sports car hung into a vicious left-hand, negative-camber turn. Right behind us was a yellow Porsche, pressing to pass on the turn. The burning rubber squealed as the Porsche drew abreast. The steering wheel slipped in my hands and we went cartwheeling over the cliff, and I awoke, sweaty and weak.

I was still confined aboard a boat crossing the gigantic mouth of the Rio del Plata, desperately trying for Uruguay. I wrote in my diary, "The past seems dead. We were turned away at Paradise, Mar del Plata. I'll never know if I could have gotten in. Maybe, but it was all against us -- 35 knots and the set. Impossible this. I was as close to death yesterday as ever. Somehow I rallied and I'm going on. The pain is still with me from the wound but I am becoming more functional. This next opportunity of Uruguay is our only and last chance. Montevideo is the most dangerous entrance I've ever seen on charts. It's lined with wrecks and obstructions and reefs.

"1800. About 90 miles out and the wind is switching and dying and flies are everywhere. I pray I don't get turned away again."

Ships and boats dotted the huge estuary and, as darkness fell, our running lights barely flickered. To save the batteries, I showed only the masthead light, trained my flashlight on the sails, and hoped for the best.

Day 126

As the pain in my back tried to disable the rest of my body, the wind silenced and *Cestus* died in the river water. Becalmed again. About 50 miles out at 6:30 that evening, we made landfall. It was far less exciting than the landfall at Cape Horn. We were well west of the marker island, Isla de Lobos, shown on the chart with a flashing beacon, a radio beacon, and a siren. We labored in the current with Punta del Este northeast of us. Our position was good if we could avoid being swept past our goal and up the coast of Uruguay.

I called the traffic control, was put on hold, and heard nothing more.

Exhausted, depleted, and running on adrenalin and the will to come in, I wrote in my diary, "Just took a good look at myself. I look like I just got out of Auschwitz, but I'm alive."

Day 127

Thank God, the wind came up in the morning and we began tacking for Punta del Este while keeping an eye out for Isla de Lobos. About 11 a.m., I spotted what looked like masts sticking out of the water. Shipwrecks to avoid. But in my profound fatigue and mixed feelings about returning to human company, this was how my prize, Punta del Este, about 15 miles away, looked in my distorted perception. Not only did the wind spring up, but it gave us a great sail toward Punta del Este. Soon Isla de Gorriti, a small, one-mile island just offshore, came into sight.

The wind rose to what the locals called a "rolling, thundering Pampero," which has wreaked havoc on sailors in these waters for ages.

In this 20-knot wind, we sailed all afternoon, back and forth off the city. I'd set the steering vane, sail a four-mile tack, reset the vane, and sail back. Using the main sail only, I hoped to figure out how to approach the harbor.

The tall masts of large yachts made the harbor unmistakable, but in my excitement and fatigue, I couldn't find the entrance. Though I had been calling the Coast Guard every hour, there was no answer. A prudent sailor wouldn't enter the harbor without local knowledge, and I decided to continue tacking and make my try in the morning. Sunset painted the buildings of Punta del Este with golden light, and I could see why it is considered one of the most beautiful resorts in Uruguay.

Setting my wind-up alarm clock, I tried to catch some

sleep so that I'd be fresh for my attempt the next morning.

Day 128

Just after midnight, my VHF radio came to life with a curious message from the communications officer for Punta del Este. As best as I could make out his Spanish, he was asking me to take full responsibility for any damage or liability if he offered me a tow into port. Wondering if that was the reason my frantic calls had elicited no response, I agreed to assume all responsibility, and fell back to sleep. The Pampero failed to dump me from the bunk.

Later, the low rumble and the acrid diesel smoke of a tugboat awakened me. It was 1 a.m. on January 28. The Coast Guard had been warned by Freddy Chans that *Cestus* was being set down on a rocky shore. Help arrived in the form of Senor Edmundo Eduardo Lopez Chabot and an inexperienced crew of three.

Senor Edmundo Eduardo Lopez Chabot hailed me in Spanish, "I'm Coco." That was convenient.

"I'm Frank Guernsey from the United States," I shouted over the wind.

Crewman Ernesto de Franchesco tossed me a line, quickly secured, but the chop twanged it like a bow string and pulled out one metal chock and then another. This was the worst damage *Cestus* sustained for the entire voyage. Finally, the line snapped. The heavy and unwieldy tug surged about, and it was all Coco could do to keep from backing into us.

Through excellent seamanship, he avoided that disaster, and at last we were attached, bending the headstay, and started for the harbor. Donning my safety harness for the first time in months, I secured myself to the mast. As I sat, the warm spray drenched me and I loved it. To my everlasting relief, the voyage had been a success.

About an hour later, we entered the harbor mouth, and suddenly the rows of 60- and 70-foot luxury yachts turned on their lights and blew their horns. The decks were lined with well-wishers waving their congratulations. As it turned out, many spectators in the harbor had been watching the drama of my futile attempts at getting in for the entire day. It was wonderful to be among humans of good heart once again.

It was the most glorious moment of my life.

Once secure in the harbor, Coco cast me off and two old gentlemen in a dinghy towed me to a mooring. Because of my injury, I couldn't attach the mooring line, but they were happy to oblige. This was the beginning of a royal welcome to Uruguay.

They stayed on for a couple of hours, chatting and explaining that Coco was a distinguished yachtsman, a member of the most exclusive yacht club in Punta del Este, and the only Uruguayan ever to sail in the Whitbread round-the-world race. All the while, we could hear music and partying coming across the water in the mild morning. My companions explained that the city was alive with music and conviviality because it was "in season."

Once they left, I tidied up dear *Cestus*. I'd soon have to face this day of re-entry. For months, I had been free, my own captain, and now I would be entering structured society. Already I realized that the voyage had changed my spirit and things had taken on a different perspective, a different meaning, and different priorities. At last I fell into a deep sleep, feeling an enormous thankfulness and relief. The one-hundred and twenty-eighth day -- the voyage was over.

* * * * * * * * * *

Awake at 8 a.m., I saw we were moored about a half-mile from the docks. The morning was superb, the day as temperate as our best in Southern California. The cloudless sky held no threat, and I felt snug in the harbor. There I was without a dinghy, but as I sat in the cockpit enjoying the morning sun, I hailed a couple on a nearby boat who were ready to row ashore. They, like many of the other yachts in the resort, were part of the South American elite on a sailing holiday, having sailed from Buenos Aires. The friendly couple spoke little English, but they were happy to take me ashore.

On my way with passport and a few dollars to the dockmaster's office, I stepped on land for the first time in 128 days. The sensation stunned me. It was as if I could feel the entire land mass of South America under my feet.

The dockmaster assured me there would be no interrogations and that I was welcome in Uruguay. My already soaring spirits rose. Two blocks away, at the dockmaster's suggestion, I checked in with the Coast Guard.

All bearing sidearms, the officers welcomed me through an enlisted man interpreter and advised I should check in with immigration. Seriously concerned with my health, they asked me to return in two hours, when they could have their doctor examine me.

The marina was near their original Old Town and was surrounded by magnificent estates. The area exuded charm and great wealth. I walked to a nearby restaurant and sat on the patio, where I drank a beer, ate a salad and watched people. The beer was the nectar of the gods and the salad reminded me of home.

My mind was hyper-aware in a spiritual sense. It was as if I could communicate with the minds of everyone walking by and absorb their thoughts. Never in my life was I more receptive to other humans. These other humans could feel the communication and the tranquillity that I was broadcasting, and they smiled. Even though I was clean as always, my beard and wrinkled shirt and shorts made it obvious that I was just off a boat. I basked in their silent good wishes.

The feeling held as I found the local barbershop. Apparently, the barber and the customers knew that I was the American who had sailed alone from North America. The men insisted that I go ahead of them, and the barber absolutely refused any payment for the haircut. This was a deeply moving experience.

Back at Coast Guard headquarters, the English-speaking

doctor diagnosed torn cartilage and broken ribs. There was no special treatment. And, luckily, my head had healed perfectly, even without stitches. The doctor's scales revealed that I had lost 30 pounds.

Soon I located immigration and, much to my relief, the only red tape was stamping my passport. I was now officially in the country.

After making arrangements to have *Cestus* towed from the mooring to the dock, I decided to take a midday walk around the point where the expensive homes were. From the heights, I could see a lone sailboat in the vast estuary beyond Lobos Island, and a forceful thanksgiving welled up in me.

For the next hour, I walked around the modern part of the city. This would probably be my most lasting memory of Punta del Este, which resembled parts of the Italian and French Riviera. I settled in at an open-air restaurant to drink a beer and eat a hamburger. After my months at sea, a hamburger seemed like a feast.

Then came the best part of being ashore: I called Mary and became ecstatic with her warmth and love. She would call my parents and Frankie. "I'll be there as soon as I can arrange a flight," she said. Those were the happiest words I had heard in a long time.

Sadly, she reported that only the Filipino captain of the ship that I had contacted about 1,000 miles off the coast of Mexico had relayed my message to her.

My second call was to Steve Peterman of the Los Angeles Adventurers' Club. Not only did I want him to report the news of my safe arrival to the other members of the club, but Steve was the most helpful Adventurer in my preparations for the voyage. Steve had helped me fiberglass over the through-holes and install the cockpit drains.

The lovely resort city and all the congenial people seemed to be part of a magical Guernseyland. Eventually, I returned to the boat to be confronted by reporters from the Uruguayan radio and print media. I had dreaded this moment, wishing to avoid it altogether.

The Uruguayan reporters were polite and civil. I was happy to see their reporting was fair and accurate. Their questions were intelligent and their accounts portrayed me in a matter-of-fact way. So I was a momentary celebrity in Uruguay and Argentina, presented in the context of an everyday adventurer.

That evening, I went to a nearby seaside restaurant, where I met its owner, Maximilian Patterson, who claimed to be the only American businessman in Uruguay. He immediately befriended me, and because of his many local connections, made my life in Uruguay easier. Though the food at Max's was delicious, I couldn't eat much. When Max eventually saw *Cestus*, he called her "the floating Thermos." He called me a "sea roamer."

The next morning, I located Coco. Later, Coco and I went out for sea trials. *Cestus* performed beautifully under his expert hand. Suitably impressed, Coco offered $3,000 American to buy *Cestus*. The little craft had been so worked that I didn't have the heart to demand more.

As we sailed, Coco remarked that he was in charge of sailing instruction at the Punta del Este Yacht Club. There is probably no more private yacht club anywhere in the world, so I envisioned good sailors enjoying my old companion for years to come.

Five more days of growing anticipation went by before Mary arrived. At our joyful reunion, Mary remarked that I was somehow different, and I had to admit to a certain degree of abstraction after the lonely voyage. The hospitable Uruguayans invited us to many spirited parties, and the city lived up to its reputation as the playboy capital of South America. The Uruguayans treated us like visiting dignitaries.

Channel 7 of Montevideo sent a reporter to our rented condo to interview Mary and me. The interview was shown in Argentina as a sports special.

Of all places to re-enter civilization after a long voyage,

Punta del Este, Uruguay, may be the best.

Max had located the condo in the Quartro Mares complex, a wonderful headquarters for us high above the other buildings with a view to the horizons in all directions. Mary had brought large duffel bags, and on the floor of the condo we made huge piles of my gear to carry back to the States.

Going back home with me were the faithful PUR watermaker, the unfailing Magellan GPS, my sextant, logs, diaries, charts, cold weather gear, videos, and cameras. Staying behind was the shotgun.

On my last day in Uruguay, I went down alone to the dock to see *Cestus* for the last time and to tell her good bye. My emotion for dear *Cestus* overwhelmed me, and I felt as if I had given away a wonderful child.

Just short of three weeks after my arrival, Mary and I boarded a bus to the Montevideo airport.

That afternoon, the incredible power of a jet lifting from the runway drove us into our seat backs, and we were on our way to New York via Buenos Aires. During the long, somber flight to New York, I felt a growing anxiety about the return to day-to-day life.

The customs official in New York just stared at me as if a wild man were seeking entry to the United States. She asked where I had been, and when I told her, she looked mystified. A long silence followed, and without searching my gear she said, "Welcome home."

Chapter Twenty

Re-Entering The
Human Race

On February 15, United Airlines flight 19 slid over
the edge of the Los Angeles Basin and began its slow descent
into Los Angeles International Airport. There were gasps from
those aboard who had never made the decline.

Rain had cleansed the air over the megalopolis. Snow
mantled the San Gabriel Mountains, and I could imagine skiers
glancing at our plane.

The sight of wall-to-wall habitations twinkling with blue

swimming pools stretching from the desert and mountains ahead to the unseen ocean was both exciting and appalling. Exciting to think about the millions of people who had crowded the basin searching for a better life, and appalling to think about what their presence has done to Southern California's fragile environment.

Down there among the millions of humans, I would have to re-establish myself, make my presence known to strangers to make my insurance business recover and expand. How would things turn out? You never know what awaits you at the other end of a voyage.

As the chipper voice of a flight attendant filled the cabin, Mary awakened and squeezed my hand.

Flights into Los Angeles seem to take hours from the edge of the city to the airport by the sea. Since we were on the port side of the aircraft, I could see Palos Verdes Peninsula to the south. I loved its familiar gray profile. Beyond the Peninsula, Santa Catalina Island posed as if for a portrait. How long ago our departure seemed, and I flashed on *Cestus* far behind.

For the first time in 46 days, I saw the Pacific Ocean, aware of Hawaii, Tahiti, and Japan far over the horizon. A bizarre wish to sail away floated through my head.

Eventually, we swooped over the Harbor Freeway, and the cars were locked in an ant-like march toward a sugar bowl. Before long, I'd be scurrying up and down those freeways with the other ants trying to make a living. The residents of Inglewood below would wait for our plane to roar over before they resumed their telephone conversations. To the south, the eight stacks of the Edison electric plant marked King Harbor Marina and our home.

We were dropping below the tops of the buildings and, in seconds, the tires smoked and squawked and the airplane, dashing down the runway, had plunged out of its environment. I felt the same way, but in an instant my ambivalence disappeared and I was excited to be home. I looked forward to redeveloping camaraderie among the local sailors, cocktails at the yacht club, running on the sand, and the other pleasures of life at the beach.

That night, Mary and I dined at the Casa Blanca restaurant, one of our favorites, in Hermosa Beach. She was interested in my story about my message in a bottle, but if people ever found it they never contacted her.

When my head hit the pillow in my own bed, I felt as if I were back at the starting point of an immense circle. *Cestus* and I had survived because of prudent sailing, good fortune, and God. I realized that though I had admired the physical courage of friends who could cope with violence offered by other humans, I had coped with the violence offered by nature. I had learned we need and must abide by the rules and being out there is trading the rules of society for the rules of nature. I prefer the rules of nature. I had learned the material ambitions that motivated me for much of my life were empty, and that providing for Mary and making her happy is my primary ambition. I came back a stronger person than the one who had sailed into the uncertainty of the Southern Ocean.

It had seemed a lifetime since I cast off from Avalon. I could hardly remember what I had hoped to gain from the voyage. What I did gain was a stronger belief in a Supreme Being and in myself. I read the entire Old and New Testaments and I lived Hebrews 12:1. "...let us lay aside every weight, and the sin which doth so easily beset us, and let us run with patience the race that is set before us." In my imagination, I could see my rival, the line of icebergs. The sea taught me the remainder of the spiritual lessons.

Physically, I had endured and because of that returned better disciplined. Any physical fears posed ashore would seem forever slight compared with the ultimate storm in the Southern Ocean.

Emotionally, I had journeyed to the edge of madness and back. And, having survived, I was better armed for the emotional roller coaster that constitutes my daily life. Sailing had endowed me with more patience and more willingness to wait for events to take their course.

Economically, I had hoped to gain nothing, and nothing was what I got. In fact, making up for the money I didn't make while I was voyaging would occupy me for years.

Content, I drifted off to sleep.

The day after my return, I drove up the coast to Santa Barbara where my son, Frank, was a senior in environmental studies at the University of California. In my absence, he had done a wonderful job of keeping up both his studies and the loose ends of my insurance business. There was actually an encouraging amount of money in the bank.

In the next few days, I visited my father, who was extremely proud of my accomplishment, and my mother, who was pleased to see me alive and in good spirits.

For the first month, I was on a honeymoon with life and the world. It was a time of celebration and good will. I enjoyed the greetings of members of the Redondo Beach Yacht Club and the characters I knew around King Harbor Marina, many of whom had not expected to see me again. This was no time for crowing, however, and I simply enjoyed the people and each day enormously.

It was hearty congratulations all around at the Adventurers' Club, where many a toast was raised to me and to the success of the voyage. My reception moved me because so many of the members I held in the highest esteem for their achievements in the world of adventure

A number of yacht clubs, including my own, requested an account of my voyage, and I worked hard editing my videotapes. Not wanting to appear like a braggart, I decided to let the tapes do the talking for me. The presentations gave me a good deal of pleasure because the audiences enjoyed them. There couldn't have been more attentive spectators.

Many local newspapers interviewed and produced accurate accounts and flattering pictures, but my favorite article was written by Garrison Frost, Jr., of The Beach Reporter, one of the two sources of hometown news in our beach cities. The article appeared under the headline "Redondo sailor returns from solo 'round the Horn' adventure."

He best captured my feeling at the time. The article began, "Just about everyone has experienced at one time or another the strange period of trying to adapt to things upon coming home from a trip. Spend a week in the mountains and you might find it hard to sit in a dry office. An airplane trip across three or four time zones is bound to leave you drowsy for a few days.

"For Redondo Beach resident Frank Guernsey the problem of getting used to being home is one of completely different proportions.

"Put simply, his was no ordinary trip. As a matter of fact his was one he sometimes didn't expect to survive...."

Frost grasped the problems of a returning solo sailor. He continued, "As he slowly rebuilds his life -- restarting his insurance business, buying a car, editing the hours of videotape he took on his trip -- Guernsey is coming to deal with the fact that while civilization changed very little in his absence, he may be a very changed man....

" 'I'm starting over,' he said, adding that this new challenge is nearly as daunting as his trip. 'Who knows what's in the cards for me?' "

In addition, an article about my voyage appeared in the newsletter of the prestigious Joshua Slocum Society, devoted to encouraging single-handed voyaging. The publication circulates to an international membership.

I made it a point of honor to track down the man who had demanded a bottle of scotch for towing me into Avalon. It was wonderful to satisfy the obsession of many months and thousands of miles, but the joke was on me. The scotch surprised him. He turned out to be a nice guy who obviously had forgotten making any comment at all.

His was probably an attempt at humor that struck me in the wrong mood. Even though I could see he had really meant nothing by his remark, I forced the scotch on him simply because he was a good man whom I had misjudged. Whatever hostility I felt for him dissolved.

Perhaps being at sea for more than 3,000 hours and experiencing raw conflict made me see hostility for others as foolishness. *Cestus*, after all, had survived by yielding to the whim of seas that would have jolted an aircraft carrier.

The honeymoon with the world ended a month after my return, almost to the day, about the time I was getting serious about resurrecting my insurance business. A member of the Adventures' Club nagged an editor of the local metropolitan newspaper to run an interview with me. I was uncertain about being interviewed but finally agreed and met the reporter.

Unexpectedly, while sitting alone in a coffee shop enjoying my breakfast, I saw the full-page story, replete with photographs. Initially, I was stunned and then read on, humiliated, embarrassed, and devastated. The distorted and inaccurate article paraded a sick version of my relationship with Mary before the public. It depicted my character as a lunatic form of Evil Knieval.

The reality that I had to earn a living to survive in my profession distracted me from brooding about the article and, in fact, the article did not appear to dampen the enthusiasm of the people who flocked to my presentations at Southern California yacht clubs, marine museums, service clubs, and schools. Everywhere I felt the good will of sailors, business people, and students.

When members of the audience asked about the most dangerous and terrifying part of the voyage, I readily responded, "the storm." The tapes really couldn't convey the terror because during the storm my hands were full trying to survive. The feeling produced by incessant danger was almost impossible to convey -- running in big seas day after day, week after week. The effect was cumulative and profound.

When audiences asked for the lowest point of the voyage, it was falling on the stanchion. The pain accompanied me for weeks into re-entry. When they asked, "What was the highest point of your trip?" of course I answered Cape Horn. Ultimately seeing the Cape from my small boat was a greater high than actually surviving the unlikely voyage. Even so, finally receiving the tow from Coco into Punta del Este was tremendously satisfying.

The worst part about returning to day-to-day life was the grim process of selling life insurance, even though I was happy to see my clients again. It seemed in my brief absence, the old ways had changed. Computers now seemed more important than people.

The insurance companies had become more difficult for salespeople to deal with. Loyalty seemed a thing of the past. Mass marketing rather than the personal touch was the new watchword. Competition grew more intense and inhuman.

The public seemed more jaded about everything, including being solicited on the telephone for insurance products.

Perhaps all this had happened before I left, but I could see it more clearly now.

Like many other businesses, insurance has a high rate of rejection. I discovered the most difficult thing about being back was the constant rejection. I spend my days listening to "no."

Despite my attempts, my business resisted resurrection with all its might. A kind of boredom set in, and I began wondering what would provide the trigger for my next voyage, if any.

Two years after my return from rounding the primordial Cape, I found myself at odds with Mary once again, alone and disillusioned, walking in the King Harbor area. There was an overcast that the locals aptly call "June gloom." It reflected my spirits perfectly because I felt more lonely than I ever had on any voyage.

By chance, I arrived at the impound dock and decided to see what boats were available. The marina business had not fully recovered since the aerospace crash a decade earlier. At one time, there was a waiting list to get a slip in the local marinas. Now there were plenty of vacancies. Sailors who were unable to keep up slip rent sometimes abandoned their boats, and eventually the marina gained the legal right to sell the derelicts in an attempt to recover the rent. While the boats waited for sale, they resided on the impound dock.

There among the other derelicts was a graceful sloop about 22 or 23 feet long. It looked even more forlorn than *Cestus* had when I first saw her. The companionway was open and it looked as if it had about half of *Cestus'* living space below. Despite years of neglect and deterioration, it caught my eye. I walked up to the office and Kevin told me it was a Pearson Electra, 22 1/2 feet long on deck, rudderless, abandoned, impounded, and for sale. Beyond that he knew nothing.

The former owner was nowhere to be found.

The prospect was intriguing -- daunting. My mind raced.

No less than a complete reconstruction of the little sloop. The base of the mast was corroded and either I could fit a new mast or cut three inches from the bottom of this one and step it on a three-inch block of wood. The missing rudder would have to be replaced. I'd probably have to design a new one because it was unlikely that patterns were available. Then a new rudder would have to be fabricated and fitted.

The graceful little sloop would need new spreaders, turnbuckles, and rigging all around. The entire boat would need rewiring. I was becoming more excited. Something would have to be done to reinforce the hull to ensure structural integrity. The decks needed a non-skid treatment. Corroded fasteners would have to be replaced. A steering vane and dodger would be desirable.

The head would have to be removed and the through-hull fittings would need to be fiberglassed over. The Electra was in desperate need of new sails. An entire list of repairs and refurbishings sprang to mind. Apparently, the boat had no name, and potentially MF for Mary and Frank sounded good.

To accomplish all these tasks, I'd have to reassemble the

whole cast of characters. I had heard that Bob Cringan was back from Costa Rica, and he'd probably be willing to lend a hand once again, along with other helpers from the *Cestus* days.

While reconstructing the boat, I could sail it in the Redondo Beach Yacht Club races to reinforce my intuition that this was a capable offshore skiff.

Walking up to the marina office, I felt my heart pound. Already, I could see distant oceans.

Kevin looked up from behind the counter as I entered the glass door.

"Would you take $100 for the Pearson?" I asked.
"Yes!"

Garrison Frost, Jr.

Frank Guernsey

Frank W. Guernsey is a world-class solo sailor. His most recent adventure, aboard a 24-foot fiberglass sloop, took him on a 128-day nonstop singlehanded voyage from Redondo Beach, California, to Punta del Este, Uruguay, via Cape Horn. In 1978, he sailed the *Boogie*, a 26-foot sloop, down the coast of Baja, California, then voyaged to Maui, Hawaii, in 1980.

Five years later, he sailed his wooden sloop *Amethyst* to Papeete, Tahiti, in 47 days. In 1988, he again set out on Amethyst, this time to Aburatsubo, Japan, which took 87 days. In all, Frank has voyaged 289 days (almost ten months) alone at sea in small sailboats. His exploits have been highlighted in the Japanese and South American media and in the local, regional, and national media in the United States.

Born in 1942 in Los Angeles, he spent his teen years in the rebel-without-a-cause Southern California culture and in the United States Marine Corps. He is a member of the Los Angeles Adventurers' Club and the Redondo Beach Yacht Club, where, in club races, he tunes for his prospective ocean voyages. When not crossing oceans alone, Frank runs an insurance business. His son Frankie manages the business during his father's voyages. Frank and his wife, Mary, live in Redondo Beach.

Frank Matranga

Cy Zoerner

Cy Zoerner (pronounced Zerner) sails and writes. Almost daily, he single-hands *Tough Ship* out of King Harbor, near his home in Manhattan Beach, California. According to his log, he has spent more than 2,000 hours alone at sea. When he's feeling adventurous, he sails his 14-foot sloop to Catalina Island, some 25 miles from his home port. Cy has crewed in the international Newport-Ensenada race and in numerous regional offshore races. Locally, he races in the Horizon Series sponsored by the Redondo Beach Yacht Club. Aboard *Jedna*, a competitive Cal 25, he trims the main sail in one-design races at the Long Beach Yacht Club

His articles have appeared in major American newspapers, magazines, and journals for more than 30 years. He wrote *Marketing First,* a successful college textbook, and has ghost written several nonfiction books. His work has appeared in *The Spray,* the publication of the Joshua Slocum Society, and in national and regional sailing magazines. Cy is considered an authority on the *Igdrasil*, a copy of Slocum's circumnavigator. He holds a doctorate from the University of Illinois.

Cy and his wife, Laura, have four children and three grandchildren.

Books published by
Bristol Fashion Publications
Free catalog, phone 1-800-478-7147

Boat Repair Made Easy — Haul Out
Written By John P. Kaufman

Boat Repair Made Easy — Finishes
Written By John P. Kaufman

Boat Repair Made Easy — Systems
Written By John P. Kaufman

Boat Repair Made Easy — Engines
Written By John P. Kaufman

Standard Ship's Log
Designed By John P. Kaufman

Large Ship's Log
Designed By John P. Kaufman

Custom Ship's Log
Designed By John P. Kaufman

Designing Power & Sail
Written By Arthur Edmunds

Fiberglass Boat Survey
Written By Arthur Edmunds

Building A Fiberglass Boat
Written By Arthur Edmunds

Buying A Great Boat
Written By Arthur Edmunds

**Outfitting & Organizing Your Boat
For A Day, A Week or A Lifetime**
Written By Michael L. Frankel

Boater's Book of Nautical Terms
Written By David S. Yetman

Modern Boatworks
Written By David S. Yetman

Practical Seamanship
Written By David S. Yetman

Captain Jack's Basic Navigation
Written By Jack I. Davis

Captain Jack's Celestial Navigation
Written By Jack I. Davis

Captain Jack's Complete Navigation
Written By Jack I. Davis

Southwinds Gourmet
Written By Susan Garrett Mason

The Cruising Sailor
Written By Tom Dove

Daddy & I Go Boating
Written By Ken Kreisler

My Grandpa Is A Tugboat Captain
Written By Ken Kreisler

Billy The Oysterman
Written By Ken Kreisler

Creating Comfort Afloat
Written By Janet Groene

Living Aboard
Written By Janet Groene

Simple Boat Projects
Written By Donald Boone

Racing The Ice To Cape Horn
Written By Frank Guernsey & Cy Zoerner

Boater's Checklist
Written By Clay Kelley

Florida Through The Islands
What Boaters Need To Know
Written By Captain Clay Kelley & Marybeth

Marine Weather Forecasting
Written By J. Frank Brumbaugh

Basic Boat Maintenance
Written By J. Frank Brumbaugh

Complete Guide To Gasoline Marine Engines
Written By John Fleming

Complete Guide To Outboard Engines
Written By John Fleming

Complete Guide To Diesel Marine Engines
Written By John Fleming

Trouble Shooting Gasoline Marine Engines
Written By John Fleming

Trailer Boats
Written By Alex Zidock

Skipper's Handbook
Written By Robert S. Grossman

Wake Up & Water Ski
Written By Kimberly P. Robinson

White Squall - The Last Voyage Of Albatross
Written By Richard E. Langford

Cruising South
What to Expect Along The ICW
Written By Joan Healy

Electronics Aboard
Written By Stephen Fishman

A Whale At the Port Quarter
A Treasure Chest of Sea Stories
Written By Charles Gnaegy

Five Against The Sea
A True Story of Courage & Survival
Written By Ron Arias

Scuttlebutt
Seafaring History & Lore
Written By Captain John Guest USCG Ret.

Cruising The South Pacific
Written By Douglas Austin

After Forty Years
How To Avoid The Pitfalls of Boating
Written By David Wheeler

Catch of The Day
How To Catch, Clean & Cook It
Written By Carla Johnson

VHF Marine radio Handbook
Written By Mike Whitehead

REVIEWS

A Bluewater Sailing top pick of 1999

The Beach Reporter
Book Review by Garrison Frost.

The book is aimed at the same readers who are flocking to buy adventure nonfiction such as Jon Krakauer's "Into Thin Air" and Sebastian Junger's "The Perfect Storm". These readers will not be disappointed by Guernsey and Zoerner's book with its description of gales, high seas and pirate ships -- of human strength and weakness in the face of the great indifference of nature.

The book also stands.... as a rare document of the South Bay known by Guernsey's generation in its youth.

The Daily Breeze
Meredith Grenier

...sail alone around the treacherous tip of Cape Horn...

At the end of his 128-day trail, he was towed half-dead into Punta del Este, Uruguay, after battling surreal storms that slammed 60- to 80-foot walls of water into his [24-foot] boat for half a week.

On clear days he dealt with pirates, malfunctions, starvation and relentless cold.

L.A.Times - South Bay
Deborah Paul

...spellbinding...

The 246 page sea adventure gives a spellbinding account of Guernsey's marathon competition against himself and the Antarctic elements.

Palos Verdes Peninsula News
Josh Cohen

Guernsey's four-month voyage took him through some of the roughest seas in the world, leaving him alone to face the dangers of capsizing, starvation, thirst, madness, pirates...   The elements, which Guernsey was quite aware of, would prove to be his most apparent foe.

Joshua Slocum Society
Ted Jones - Commodore

Read it immediately and have been numbed by the height of Frank's experience on the voyage. Never thought that we could feel what he felt, but we did.

It was impossible to put down, once we started the venture.

Reader Reviews

Texas

..."truth is stranger than fiction"...
...an unlikely hero...
Great Read

Colorado

The book hooks you after a few pages, and you never feel like putting it down.

...I loved it...

California

This book is unbelievable...

I personally recommend this book to anyone who likes tales of adventure.

Arizona

Enthralling! I couldn't put it down.

I can warmly recommend this book to sailors and non-sailors alike - it's exciting!